OECD Urban Studies

Improving Transport Planning for Accessible Cities

Please cite this publication as:
OECD (2020), *Improving Transport Planning for Accessible Cities*, OECD Urban Studies, OECD Publishing, Paris, *https://doi.org/10.1787/fcb2eae0-en*.

ISBN 978-92-64-93959-2 (print)
ISBN 978-92-64-59356-5 (pdf)

OECD Urban Studies
ISSN 2707-3432 (print)
ISSN 2707-3440 (online)

Photo credits: Cover © panimoni/Gettyimages.com.

Corrigenda to publications may be found on line at: *www.oecd.org/about/publishing/corrigenda.htm*.

Foreword

The COVID-19 pandemic has had a profound impact on our daily lives, and in particular on our mobility, with increased up-take of digitalisation at the forefront. On-going megatrends such as teleworking and e-commerce have accelerated, raising questions about the type of transport infrastructure we have in place today and that we need, in an uncertain, tomorrow.

The promise of a new vaccine provides hope of a return to normality and some degree of clarity of what tomorrow might look like but it is already clear that many of the changes accelerated by the pandemic are likely to remain in the 'new normal', especially those that have been welfare and productivity enhancing, as firms have invested in new technologies and digital infrastructures, and consumers have shifted their habits.

But much of the new normal will look like the old normal: many jobs require physical presence and many (especially personal, medical, and recreational) services cannot be delivered digitally. Efficient transport infrastructure remains as important today, and indeed tomorrow, as it has always been, especially as a tool to avoid new forms of digital-divide emerging but also to ensure that we continue to make our regions and cities attractive places to live and work.

This means that we must be proactive in our thinking, especially in respect of the diversity of mobility solutions, and how they can adapt to COVID-19 challenges as well as challenges that were with us before COVID-19, for example with respect to diverse demographic changes across cities, with some growing larger and some smaller, and some growing older.

Whilst the current pandemic has given greater urgency to dealing with these challenges, it has also created greater awareness about the importance of well-being and social cohesion and sustainable economic growth in the way that we shape our policies. The success of cities in providing access to opportunities for all will shape how inclusive cities are, as will greening of urban transport, which will be important in contributing to efforts towards carbon neutrality and sustainability.

Improving transport planning for accessible cities highlights that transport investment on its own does not suffice to promote access to opportunities for everyone. While cities need to focus on transit-oriented development, putting public transport and "active mobility" at the heart of transport strategies, with effective governance mechanisms to align different planning frameworks, is critical to help make better use of urban transport infrastructure. A companion report *OECD Urban Studies: Transport Bridging Divides* focuses on the economic benefits of transport infrastructure in general, and the measurement and analysis of access to opportunities within cities in particular.

This report was developed as part of the Programme of Work and Budget of the Regional Development Policy Committee, supporting its agenda to promote productivity, inclusion and resilience within and across regions and cities. The project benefited from the financial support from the European Commission's Directorate-General for Regional and Urban Policy (DG REGIO) as part of a wider project on 'Rethinking urban and regional transport needs: improving access, safety and well-being through transport investment and policies'.

Acknowledgements

This report was produced by the OECD Centre for Entrepreneurship, SMEs, Regions and Cities (CFE) led by Lamia Kamal-Chaoui, Director. It is part of the Programme of Work of the OECD's Regional Development Policy Committee (RDPC).

The report was prepared as part of a wider project on *Rethinking urban and regional transport needs: improving access, safety and well-being through transport investment and policies*, jointly implemented by the CFE and the OECD's International Transport Forum (ITF). The financial contributions from the Directorate-General for Regional and Urban Policy (DG REGIO) and the support and feedback received at various stages of the project by Lewis Dijkstra are gratefully acknowledged.

The OECD Secretariat would like to thank the numerous local officials and experts that met with the OECD team and provided valuable insights in Madrid, Prague, Vancouver and Romania. In particular, the Secretariat is grateful to Andrew Devlin, Andew McCurran and Kyle Rosenke from TransLink and Heather McNell and James Stiver from Metro Vancouver (Canada); Laura Delgado Fernández and Francisco Javier López Gómez from the Consorcio Regional de Transportes de Madrid (Spain); Jaromír Hainc and Kristina Kleinwachterová from the Prague Institute of Planning and Development (Czech Republic), and Liviu Băileșteanu and Radu Necsuliu from the Ministry of Regional Development of Romania for their kind assistance in organising the study missions and providing valuable information for the report and case studies.

The report was drafted by Oscar Huerta Melchor, Policy Analyst in the Cities, Urban Policies and Sustainable Development Division, CFE, with inputs from Federica Daniele, Alexander C. Lembcke, Abel Schumann, Antonio Cañamás Catalá and Jared Gars. Alexander C. Lembcke coordinated the overall project under the supervision of Rudiger Ahrend, Head of the Economic Analysis, Statistics and Multi-level Governance section in CFE. Charles Victor and Jeanette Duboys provided administrative support throughout the project's implementation phase.

This report was submitted to delegates for approval by written procedure by 27 November 2020 under the cote CFE/RDPC/URB(2020)21. The final version was edited and formatted by Eleonore Morena and received editorial inputs by Alexandra Taylor. Pilar Philip prepared the manuscript for publication.

Table of contents

Tables

Figures

Boxes

Executive summary

Developing accessible cities – where people can connect easily with jobs, services, goods and other people – is essential to economic prosperity, social development and environmental sustainability. Policy-makers increasingly acknowledge that a first key step in this direction is to move from a planning model that focuses on mobility to one that connects people to local amenities. The COVID-19 pandemic has exacerbated the need for this change by reasserting the importance of proximity to the means by which people access social, economic and cultural opportunities. The current context presents a window of opportunity to adopt policies for a compact and connected urban growth, but also a challenge as governments may adopt economic recovery measures that may derail progress already made, for example, relaxing environmental standards to allow energy providers to operate and granting subsidies for buying cars.

A return to business-as-usual would run the risk of deepening pre-existing inequalities in cities as low-income-households have less access to opportunities than more affluent ones. In metropolitan areas where access is the least inclusive, residents of high-income neighbourhoods live surrounded on average by almost twice as many opportunities than residents of low-income neighbourhoods. Moreover, promoting accessibility is a way of contributing to environmental goals as it can reduce the need for mobility or make travel more efficient, thus resulting in lower emissions. While improving accessibility, cities can make low-carbon travel the default option.

To build accessible cities policy-makers need to act in four interlinked areas: public transport performance, urban form, cross-sectoral planning, and governance.

First, urban accessibility requires improving the performance of the public transport network -greater capacity, increased speed and/or higher frequency - accompanied by efforts to increase proximity between people and opportunities. This could be achieved by adopting a series of policies that favour a liveable level of density (which emphasises quality of life) and mixed land-use. Another option is by building an intermodal and integrated transport system. While an *intermodal* transport system ensures that all means of transport complement each other, such as Madrid's intermodal interchanges, an *integrated* transport system, like in Prague and Warsaw, makes travel easier and more affordable for commuters by encouraging the use of public transport. A highly performing public transport system requires active mobility initiatives (walking and cycling), which are the fastest, least expensive, and space-efficient mode of door-to-door travel for short distances. In Copenhagen, for example, taking a bicycle results in a net profit for society of DKK 3.65 (USD 0.58), while taking a car results in a net loss for society of DKK 6.59 (USD 1.04). Cities need to re-allocate space for walking and cycling and build the necessary infrastructure using the momentum created by the COVID-19 pandemic and creating linkages to long-term accessibility objectives. Moreover, smart city projects can potentially improve the performance of the transport network and enhance accessibility, such as Finland's Mobility as a Service (MaaS) projects that seek to take advantage of (digital) technologies to boost well-being and provide more efficient transport services.

Second, enhancing accessibility requires improving urban form (i.e. size, shape, and configuration) that increases social cohesion and promotes well-being in urban areas. It requires ensuring a sufficient level of density to make the most of the agglomeration benefits; integrating land-use and transport policies through transit-oriented development strategies; building pedestrian-friendly cities to improve connectivity, i.e. building infrastructure; and offering different transport options, i.e. public transport, walking and cycling to reach a destination, such as in London, Milan and Stuttgart.

Third, fostering accessibility needs promoting synergies across social, economic and environmental aspects for urban development. The aim is to ensure that planning the city's movement and transport contributes to building accessible and attractive cities, as in Gothenburg's transport strategy, for example. This requires both the national planning framework to set goals and outline a general vision for spatial development, and subnational governments to operationalise national transport priorities through a transport strategy that seeks to improve transport services, redesign existing neighbourhoods, and build transit-oriented communities (TOCs). By design, TOCs allow people to drive less and walk, cycle and take public transport more often, as in the Metro Vancouver Regional District. However, TOCs may create equity challenges by favouring individuals and families who are able to pay the extra premium to live in valuable real estate close to rapid transit. A transport policy that seeks to improve accessibility requires strong linkages to housing policy under a transit-oriented affordable housing approach. One of the risks of densification is that the price of housing close to public transport stations tends to rise to the point that the only people who can afford to live near those stations are the least likely to depend on it. Thus, expanding the offer of affordable housing that benefit different socio-economic groups in areas close to public transport hubs may be necessary.

And fourth, accessible cities require more ambitious and coherent transport and urban policy actions based on a sound governance framework. It ensures a stable institutional framework, reliable sources of funding, governmental capacity and community engagement. It enables coordination across ministries, city departments and levels of government. Transport can greatly contribute to regional integration by connecting different cities through a regional transport network. In metropolitan areas, urban accessibility requires the joint action of the different municipalities. To facilitate the planning and implementation of the transport strategy in metropolitan areas, a metropolitan transport authority is often given the mandate of organising and/or providing transport services, for example: Île-de-France Mobilités, the Regional Organiser of Prague Integrated Transport, and Transport for London.

Cities need a sustainable financial framework to promote urban accessibility projects. Funding transport projects accounts for almost 40% of subnational investment across OECD countries in 2016. Many cities apply a combination of fares, dedicated taxes, and subsidies by municipal or higher levels of government. Local authorities need to explore different potential sources of funding for transport infrastructure and services. Some options include granting more financial powers to cities to diversify their revenue generation activities such as London's proposal to seek additional taxes and financial powers; land-value capture mechanism like the betterment tax in Hong Kong, China, the accessibility increment contribution such as the one implemented in Belo Horizonte, Brazil; the creation of public partnerships for transport investment such as those adopted in Vancouver, Canada; and mobilising private sector funding as in Chile.

Cities require greater capacity and capability to implement their public transport plans and achieve their accessibility objectives. Investing in a talented workforce in the administration and in the transport authority, which could take the form of a specific recruitment initiative, such as the New York City (NYC) Department of Transportation's Next Generation Programme, is key to plan accessible cities. Developing the ability to exploit the power of data is another key factor in improving capacity for developing long-term transport plans, such as smart traffic management in Stockholm, and conducting ex-post assessments of urban plans and transport strategies as in Malmö, through its Accessibility Index criteria.

Promoting dialogue with and engagement of a wider set of stakeholders helps identify preferences and build support for transport strategies and investment decisions. This is the aim of initiatives such as the NYC Department of Transportation's Vision Zero Outreach, Sydney's Future Transport Campaign, and Vancouver's community engagement practices.

1 Improving access to opportunities in cities

This chapter makes the case for enhancing urban accessibility in cities as a way to build compact, greener and more inclusive cities with higher levels of well-being. It argues that urban accessibility also has the potential to support recovery efforts from the COVID-19 pandemic via transit-oriented policies. The chapter begins with a discussion on the shift from mobility to accessibility. This is followed by an examination of the policy actions cities may consider to improve sustainable access to opportunities for everyone, in particular low-income households and women, such as improvements to the transport network, housing policies, active and micro mobility as well as smart mobility projects. The chapter concludes with a discussion on how cities can improve quality of life through the urban form by exploring urban density, land use policies, connectivity and a better balance between modes of transport.

Key messages

Cities are changing their approach to transport and urban planning to improve economic efficiency, well-being levels and environmental protection. This new approach gives more emphasis to planning for people and places rather than private cars. Easing the way people access jobs, goods and services by public transport or active mobility (walking and cycling) is a key feature of compact, connected, greener and inclusive cities. The COVID-19 pandemic has exacerbated this shift that reasserts the importance of proximity to the means by which people satisfy their needs (opportunities).

Key takeaways for national and subnational policymakers are:

- Transport investment needs to be combined with complementary policies to improve access to opportunities, in particular for low-income households and vulnerable groups. Improving accessibility requires not only an efficient public transport network but also a mix of land use, housing and other urban-related policies.
- Accessibility requires a transit-oriented, affordable-housing approach that promotes the expansion of the offer of affordable housing in central areas and closer to transit hubs. Ensuring access to public transport and creating high-density, mixed-used places where local amenities are at a short distance are critical elements to improve well-being and inclusive cities.
- Building intermodal and integrated transport systems with car parking near transport hubs is an effective manner to improve the performance of the transport system. While an intermodal transport system ensures that all transport means complement each other, an integrated transport system makes travel easier and more affordable for commuters encouraging transport use.
- Encouraging and facilitating active mobility (walking and cycling) is an effective manner to complement the public transport system and potentiate green urban transport. Active mobility is the fastest and least expensive mode for many short-distance trips, but cities require to make more efficient and safer use of streets by re-allocating space to allow walking and cycling.
- Micromobility (e-micromobility) – the use of assisted mobility devices such as e-bikes and motorised scooters – is an alternative to public transport due to their flexibility and low operating costs. Cities require investing in building safe and inclusive on-street infrastructure and issue clear regulations on what constitutes micromobility and how it can be used.
- Smart mobility projects can enhance urban accessibility and reduce the negative externalities related to transport through the use of new (digital) technologies. Shared mobility, autonomous vehicles and shared mobility schemes are the next game-changer in urban mobility but require clear government guidance to ensure they contribute to the pursuits of inclusive and accessible cities.
- Accessibility needs to be planned and fostered through a gender lens. The design, function and use of the transport system and urban environments should be planned considering the needs of all travellers equally to give everyone access to their city.
- A well-designed urban form may be an effective tool to improve accessibility, increase social cohesion and promote well-being in urban areas. It requires: ensuring a sufficient level of density to make the most of the agglomeration benefits; integrating land use and transport policies through transit-oriented development strategies; building the infrastructure for pedestrian-friendly cities to improve connectivity; and offering different mobility alternatives (transport solutions) by promoting public transit, walking and cycling.

Understanding urban accessibility

Urbanisation and transport – The background

The global urban population continues to grow unabated. Metropolitan areas account for the strongest urban population growth. Two hundred years ago, only 3% of the world's population lived in cities. Since 2007, more people live in cities than in rural areas for the first time ever, giving rise to what is known as the metropolitan century (OECD, 2015[1]). Nowadays, 48% of the world's population live in cities, 24% in rural areas and 28% in towns and semi-dense areas (OECD/European Commission, 2020[2]). The most visible expression of urbanisation lies in the so-called megacities. They represent the most densely populated urban agglomerations on earth with 10 million or more inhabitants. Megacities are economic powerhouses and form hubs which are strongly integrated into the global network of goods, capital and data flow.

With the rapid population increase, cities are reaching capacity. They register a large demand for housing and correspondingly high property prices, congested transport routes and social challenges. The more people live together in a restricted space, the more difficult it becomes to transport them from A to B. There are also different forms of transport available that also differ in the amount of space they require, their CO_2 emissions, flexibility, costs and speed. The question of which form of transport is the best choice for which person and which journey is constantly changing. There are no general solutions for all cities as there are differences in planning and socio-economic development and the established structures are too complex.

In this context of the COVID-19 pandemic, improving access to goods, services, information and people in cities contributes to economic recovery, growth and development as well as citizens' well-being and quality of life. The more efficient the access to opportunities, the greater the economic benefits through economies of scale, agglomeration effects and networking advantages. Better accessibility may imply having to travel less and in a more efficient way; this may save time and contribute to environmental protection. Managing without a car is likely to become easier in major city centres as they are normally well served by a network of trains, buses, metros and trams. However, in suburban areas, most citizens still need their own form of transport to be sufficiently mobile.

Urban accessibility is a key feature of a compact city – a spatial form characterised by 'compactness' (OECD, 2012[3]). Compact cities can take different forms but according to OECD research they have three main characteristics (2012[3]). First, compact cities have dense and proximate development patterns, which refers to how intensively urban land is utilised, and proximity concerns the location of urban agglomerations in a metropolitan area. Second, in a compact city urban areas are linked by public transport systems, which indicates how effectively urban land is utilised. Public transport systems enable urban area to function effectively. And third, in compact cities there is accessibility to local services and jobs. This refers to how easily residents can reach local services and jobs either on foot or using public transport.

COVID-19 started a debate on the vulnerability of densely populated cities as the likelihood to spread the virus is higher due to close proximity among residents making it difficult to apply physical distancing measures. However, the experience of OECD countries and cities suggests that density alone is not the problem, but the structural economic, and social conditions of cities is what makes them more or less vulnerable and enable to implement effective policy responses (OECD, 2020[4]). Cities marked with inequalities, inefficient public transport services and low urban accessibility are more vulnerable than those that are better resources, less crowded, more equal, and have higher levels of accessibility to services and jobs.

Urban accessibility can be promoted through different measures. Efficiency in transport accessibility is normally based on compact and public transport-oriented policies. It may involve retrofitting and densification of established urban areas and the promotion of transit-oriented urban expansion, mostly in areas where there is already high density. Focusing on accessibility may be considered as part of an evolutionary process in urban and transport planning but accessibility cannot be achieved without sound mobility plans, regional development plans, mixed land use plans, environmental plans and even socio-economic plans. According to research, strategies to enhance urban accessibility would normally seek to: reduce the travel intensity in cities through greater physical proximity and co-location of different urban functions; shift from private motorised modes of transport to share non-motorised modes of transport; and improve the efficiency of road-based vehicles (Rode et al., 2014[5]). And the promotion of these objectives will have to be based on sound institutional structures and planning processes as well as on effective governance arrangements.

From mobility to accessibility

Cities are changing their approach to transport and urban planning

For a long time, urban and transport planners have put a lot of emphasis on mobility when discussing the role of transport in social and economic development. Mobility refers to the ability to move freely but this is only valuable if that person can reach important destinations using their mobility (Marks, Mason and Oliveira, 2016[6]). Thus, the quest for sustainability is leading cities across OECD member and partner countries to transit from mobility-enhancing to accessibility-oriented strategies for sustainable urban planning (Gil Solá, Vilhelmson and Larsson, 2018[7]; Straatemeier, 2008[8]). This is a shift in urban planning, from viewing car transport as the means to reach services and activities distributed in the urban space to policies enabling local living and supporting environmentally friendly transport modes: public transit, cycling and walking. Planners and researchers consider accessibility planning as a key strategy to maximise the environmental sustainability and quality of life in urban areas (Coppola and Papa, 2013[9]). However, the term accessibility has been misinterpreted or poorly defined, and on many occasions is used as a synonym for mobility. The problem is that this promotes a bias towards car-oriented planning by favouring physical movement without taking into consideration the role of land use policies in improving accessibility (ITF, 2019[10]).

Accessibility planning is understood across the literature as the re-orientation of the urban structure by focusing development on places with high accessibility and making public and private transport systems more efficient (Curtis, 2008[11]; Coppola and Papa, 2013[9]). A critical difference between mobility and accessibility planning stems from the fact that former focuses on improving transport networks performance while the latter aims at maximising the access to opportunities such as workplaces, services, entertainment, education, goods and culture, for instance. However, mobility planning cannot be dissociated from accessibility as improving “access” depends largely on the performance and quality of the transport system; but its ultimate goal is not just “movement” but “access” to goods and services. Research suggests that “… [accessibility] planning should be based on the desired level of connectivity between urban functions and improving the quality of life rather than on predictions of future levels of congestion” (Inturri et al., 2017, p. 3273[12]). The focus shifts from the means (transport networks and mobility) to the ends (i.e. working studying, shopping) (Coppola and Papa, 2013[9]; Gil Solá, Vilhelmson and Larsson, 2018[7]).

Urban accessibility can be defined as the ease by which people have access to jobs, housing, shopping and in general to goods and services. It combines the proximity of opportunities and the efficiency of the transport network and therefore depends on both land use mix and the transport system. Focusing on accessibility allows linking transport planning to what people do and how private sector actors operate. Improving accessibility requires trade-offs among land use, transport options, the availability of opportunities at different times and people’s needs and abilities (Rode et al., 2019[13]). Several indicators can be used to measure accessibility, such as population, job accessibility by car or transit, access to retail or leisure opportunities, or access to green space. Highly accessible communities, particularly in compact cities such as those in Europe, are typically characterised by low daily commuting distances and travel times, enabled by multiple modes of public transport (IPCC, 2014[14]).

Planning for accessibility signals a shift from planning which focuses on the efficiency of the transport network to planning which focuses on the position and development potential of places in the wider network of cities (Straatemeier, 2008[8]). The key question planners need to answer is how to develop places in the metropolitan area that offer people and firms the means to reach more opportunities with less mobility.

A key difference is between planning for cars and planning for people and places. Accessibility, in a way, suggests that, for households and firms, the transport system itself is not important but rather the fact that it can provide them with access to spatially and temporally dispersed opportunities (Straatemeier, 2008[8]). Socio-economic changes, changing public attitudes and even technological innovations have triggered this change. Moreover, some cities have issued legislation on mobility stating the right to mobility. For example, Mexico City's Mobility Law states that residents have the right to mobility through the different transport means to satisfy their needs and that the focus of mobility should be the individual (Mexico City Government, 2014[15]).

This transition is a break from traditional transport planning. In the 1960s, transport planners used to solve urban transport problems through the classic deductive approach (data collection, defining goals and objectives, forecasting future demands). The main feature of this approach was that land use was considered a given. Planners did not advocate land use change to make the transport system more effective. In the 1980s, planners concluded that, to ensure sustainable mobility with more energy-efficient and climate-proof transport systems, a new approach was needed (Inturri et al., 2017[12]). Thus, they began to address issues of urban environmental sustainability by linking land use and transport planning (Curtis, 2008[11]).

Planning strategies could be developed to foster accessibility within the city or even region. In this way, accessibility can be used as a policy design tool to pursue broader economic, social and environmental goals, which are at the heart of present-day national and local policy discussions. The need to provide people with access to jobs or to provide firms with access to skilled workers are just some examples of these issues (Straatemeier, 2008[8]).

The shift to accessibility should not be taken for granted

Although there seems to be a shift towards enhancing accessibility as a new approach for improving lifestyle in cities, some metropolitan areas are still largely focused on mobility per se. Indeed, planning regulations and standards often support mobility rather than accessibility improvements. This is not a weakness in itself but it signals that, in some cases, planners and policymakers focus more on improving the provision and performance of the public transport system than on providing a more holistic or comprehensive solution to urban accessibility challenges. This focus could be based on a lack of interaction between agencies, e.g. the transport authority defines the mobility plans with little or no participation of the regional or metropolitan planning authority. In this situation, the transport authority has only the mandate to work on its domain. Policy-makers rarely promote new investments to foster accessibility; instead, projects are pitched based on their expected ability to reduce congestion, shorten travel times or meet projected increases in vehicle travel, focusing on the level of service and not on accessibility (Duranton and Guerra, 2016[16]). The Transportation Strategy of New York City, for instance, has a specific goal to expand mobility to sustain the city's growth (NYC Department of Transportation, 2016[17]). There is no mention of how land use and transport policies could be better linked to achieving other objectives such as providing more affordable housing in central areas. In the Madrid region, the transport strategy is not linked to other urban development because there is no regional development authority nor a regional development strategy that guides economic, land use, transport, housing and environment policy at the regional scale. In Spain, the Sustainable Urban Mobility Plan is the main planning tool for setting mobility policies at the urban level in the Madrid region. A key feature of this plan is that it gives priority to managing travel demand by increasing the volume and capacity of the transport system but not to how people could access goods and services.

The strong focus on mobility suggests that cities are still giving a lot of importance to the means and not to the end (the access to goods and services). Undoubtedly, people want to move faster, safely and comfortably, which are the features any transport system should have. However, people do not use public transport for the pleasure of doing it but because they need to get to a destination where they can access opportunities. Accessibility does not necessarily imply movement; information and communication technology (ICT) can in many cases provide access to services and goods without people needing to leave their homes. Accessibility in cities depends on the creation of the conditions for a more balanced modal split. The transport system should be designed in a way that more people regardless of age, disability, gender and socio-economic background can have access to.

It may be argued that mobility policies allow cities to focus on immediate problems, facilitating the movement of people by ordering transport, traffic and moving more people across the city. But the case studies developed by the OECD in cities such as Madrid, Prague and Vancouver suggest that if mobility policies are to be effective, they need to be complemented and co-ordinated with other urban development policies such as housing, land use, economic development and the environment. Mobility alone may not be sufficient to ensure the sustainability of urban development.

Improving (sustainable) access for everyone

In the majority of the 32 European metropolitan areas in England (United Kingdom, UK), France, Italy and Spain, low-income households benefit less from access to opportunities than high-income households, largely because of differences in the way opportunities are distributed across cities. The ratio between the average number of opportunities in an 8 km radius around a neighbourhood for high-income and low-income neighbourhoods is higher in metropolitan areas where high-income households enjoy better accessibility. In metropolitan areas where access is the least inclusive, residents of high-income neighbourhoods live surrounded on average by almost twice as many opportunities than residents of low-income neighbourhoods (Table 1.1). This ratio is less than one in metropolitan areas featuring inclusive access to opportunities, implying that residents of low-income neighbourhoods have more opportunities close to them than residents of high-income neighbourhoods. Although better transport performance alone (i.e. more frequent service on public transport or faster travel speeds) do not help to overcome accessibility gaps, there are currently no other systematic differences between neighbourhoods of different income levels that would widen those gaps. Nowadays proximity of people to opportunities is the most promising way of bridging accessibility gaps. To leverage the potential of transport performance in improving accessibility levels, investment into transport infrastructure needs to be more targeted towards those neighbourhoods particularly penalised by the uneven distribution of opportunities in cities.

Table 1.1. Inclusiveness and the distribution of opportunities in metropolitan areas

Ratio between average proximity in high-income and low-income neighbourhoods

Metropolitan areas where richer neighbourhoods have better car and public transport accessibility	1.9
Metropolitan areas where richer neighbourhoods have better accessibility by public transport but not by car	1.2
Metropolitan areas where richer and poorer neighbourhoods have similar levels of accessibility	0.9
Metropolitan areas where poorer neighbourhoods have better car and public transport access	0.7

Note: The threshold for "better" accessibility in Income Group A with respect to Income Group B is at least 25% higher accessibility in Group A compared to Group B, i.e. a large difference between the 2 groups. Average proximity in high- and low-income neighbourhoods corresponds to the number of shops located in the surrounding 8 km of an average neighbourhood, where the average is population-weighted. Transport data refers to 2018 and income data to the closest year available.
Source: Data on transport accessibility are from ITF (2019[18]), "Benchmarking Accessibility in Cities: Measuring the Impact of Proximity and Transport Performance", https://doi.org/10.1787/4b1f722b-en.

Transport investment needs to be combined with complementary policies for it to be effective at improving accessibility for everyone. Based on the analysis presented in this report, improvements in the performance of the transport system do not seem to translate into better accessibility for low-income residents and can therefore be accompanied by complementary policies such as the densification of the commercial offer in low-income neighbourhoods. However, this solution appears less viable for activities that by their own nature require a higher degree of localisation, e.g. jobs. For these activities, transport investment – accompanied by measures aimed at preserving housing affordability – remains an effective way to improve low-income families' accessibility.

Improvements in the performance of the transport network

The performance of the existing public transport network can be enhanced by means of greater capacity, increased speeds or higher frequency:

1. One example of public transport capacity improvements is the replacement of single-decker vehicles with double-decker ones. This is the case of the famous fleet of London buses or Ouigo high-speed trains in France.
2. Speed improvements are not always easy to operationalise, especially when public transport vehicles circulate in mixed traffic. The creation of dedicated bus lanes can be an effective way to improve public transport speed performance.
3. Frequency improvements can also raise the efficiency of the existing network. However, there exists a natural limit beyond which further increases in frequency can pose safety concerns. Improvements in speed help relax the constraints imposed on public transport frequency by safety concerns. Improvements in speed and frequency should therefore be seen as complementary.

Network expansion can enhance public transport performance. In cities that are reaching saturation of their local public transport network, such as in the city centre of Paris, transport policy should pursue a double objective consisting of: i) investing in alternative transport modes such as walking, cycling or micromobility in the city centre (see below); and ii) developing and/or strengthening the public transport network infrastructure in the commuting zone. These investments should aim at complementing the radial structure of the public transport system that characterises several cities with ring-type connections reducing the extent of disconnection between peripheral neighbourhoods.

Transport investment alone is not sufficient for closing accessibility gaps between rich and poorer neighbourhoods and needs to be accompanied by efforts to improve proximity for everyone. If in the surrounding neighbourhoods there are few opportunities for residents, access to opportunities will remain low in spite of a potentially perfectly operational public transport system.

Increasing the proximity of people and opportunities

A mix of policies favouring densification around newly developed infrastructure and mixed land use can increase the proximity of people and opportunities. Densification policies need to account for the growing scarcity of public space, especially in city centres. Relaxing height regulations provide the opportunity to obtain densification without necessarily reducing the amount of public space in city centres. Greater progress in this direction can be achieved by OECD member countries, whose city centre density tends to be higher on average (ITF, 2017[19]), as opposed to non-member countries.

Densification policies require a great amount of co-ordination with transport infrastructure development and co-ordination should accompany all stages of this development, from planning to execution. For instance, *ex ante* co-ordination can help avoid low-density development in an area designated by the public authorities to become a public transport hub. *Ex post* co-ordination should instead focus on orienting private developers' efforts towards areas that were recently subject to public transport performance improvements (OECD, 2017[20]).

Mixed land use refers to a situation in which different land uses, e.g. residential, commercial or industrial, are co-located. Mixed land use reduces commuting time by reducing the need for long-distance commuting in the first place and favours the adoption of transport modes different from private cars, such as walking, cycling or public transport. Mixed land use requires a strategy for inducing different types of activities to locate in the same area. The strategy can also be triggered by the development of new transport infrastructure: there are examples of cases where investments into local transport infrastructure revived local business dynamism by attracting new businesses. Policymakers seeking to increase the availability of certain amenities in given areas (e.g. shops, bars, restaurants, etc.) need to be ready to adopt complementary policies mitigating the potential subsequent increase in housing costs, owing to the fact that high-income residents might prefer living closer to these amenities.[1]

Ageing will make mixed land use increasingly important. Given that mobility of older people is limited, policies favouring greater nearness between people and opportunities can be an effective tool to improve accessibility and well-being for everybody, without leaving behind the rising share of older people in the population. For example, mixed land use in the form of so-called "complete communities" is a pillar of Calgary's Municipal Development Plan, developed in 2009 to support the 100-year vision established in 2006 by the city of Calgary, imagineCALGARY. ImagineCALGARY is the response to the growing need for sustainable urban development and mounting societal challenges in the distribution of well-being, including demographic pressures induced by the steady decline in immigration that the city has witnessed in recent decades (OECD, 2015[21]).

Accessibility for everyone requires a "transit-oriented affordable housing" approach

Transport policy that seeks to improve the accessibility of disadvantaged areas, for example by adding additional public transport routes, might not create benefits for current residents. Depending on how accessibility changes, land values in the area subject to public transport ameliorations will rise and high-income residents will outbid low-income ones, who might be therefore be forced to move out as the overall cost of housing rises. If low-income households own the property they live in, the gains in property prices accrue directly to them even if they decide to sell and move to other parts of the city (or another city altogether).[2] But those who rent will not see the same gains. The price rise can be however an opportunity for governments to collect funds to support the infrastructure development itself and complementary projects supporting the local community.[3]

Transport and housing policies are highly linked as fundamental elements of the urban system. The price of housing varies depending on its proximity to public transport and rapid transit services.[4] In Metro Vancouver, following transportation, the lack of affordable housing is one of the most frequently mentioned issues of growing concern for citizens. When housing and transportation costs are combined, the cost burden relative to the median pre-tax income is 40% for owners and 49% for renters, while low-income households can spend up to 67% of their pre-tax income on housing and transport costs (Metro Vancouver, 2015[22]). Thus, understanding the pattern and linkages of housing affordability and public transport is important to support the formulation of measures to foster accessibility. The affordability of daily travel, especially for lower-income groups, is associated with the households' housing location choice. In many metropolitan areas, households make trade-offs by either choosing more affordable housing in less accessible areas with higher commuting costs (in monetary and time terms) or spending more on housing in highly accessible areas with lower transport costs. Housing and transport affordability depend on factors such as the journey to work, vehicle ownership, the quality of local transport options, income, housing locations (Dewita, Burke and Yen, 2019[23]). Affordability also depends on the quality of infrastructure such as road design. Thus, accessibility is dependent on the location of services (schools, hospitals, shopping centres, etc.) and jobs. How all these elements are combined will determine the share of the households' budget dedicated to transport and housing. In the United States (US), for instance, households spend almost 20% of their income on housing and 11% on transportation. Housing and transportation are two of the four main categories of household expenditures in the US (Figure 1.1).

One of the measures cities adopt to improve accessibility while providing affordable transport and housing is to improve access to public transport. For this, city authorities aim to ensure that all new development is suitably located where there is good access to public transport. Residential, commercial and other developments are expected to encourage walking, cycling and the use of public transport. This is in line with the Healthy Streets Approach adopted in London. The reason is that developing locations with public transport access creates high-density, mixed-used places, where local amenities should be at short distance encouraging walking and cycling. It is expected that people living in more densely populated and developed places are more likely to use public transport, walk or cycle.

Achieving affordable housing and transport also requires creating high-density, mixed-used places. As the experience of the Île-de-France region suggests, the land around stations provides opportunities to create high-density, mixed-use places that are well connected to local services and amenities as well as jobs and locations further afield. The city of Malmö's mobility strategy suggests that providing inhabitants and commuters with the possibility to travel more sustainably requires growing and developing locations with good accessibility to public transport, infrastructure for bicycles and an attractive environment for pedestrians (City of Malmö, 2016[24]). This is a way to increase value for money and make the most of past investments in public transport infrastructure and enhance the benefits of any new investment. High-density developments, as planned in London and Vancouver, that are further away from stations can be supported by bus services and cycle lanes. Such networks can increase the catchment area of a station, provide greater employment opportunities and reduce car dependency. A city's growth potential is normally concentrated in its central business districts and town centres. Thus, as the experience of London suggests, maximising the capacity of the public transport network, extending the network to open up new areas for homes, optimising land use around stations and improving conditions for walking and cycling are means to use transport to support growth (Greater London Authority, 2018[25]).

Figure 1.1. Household consumption expenditures in the United States, 2002-19

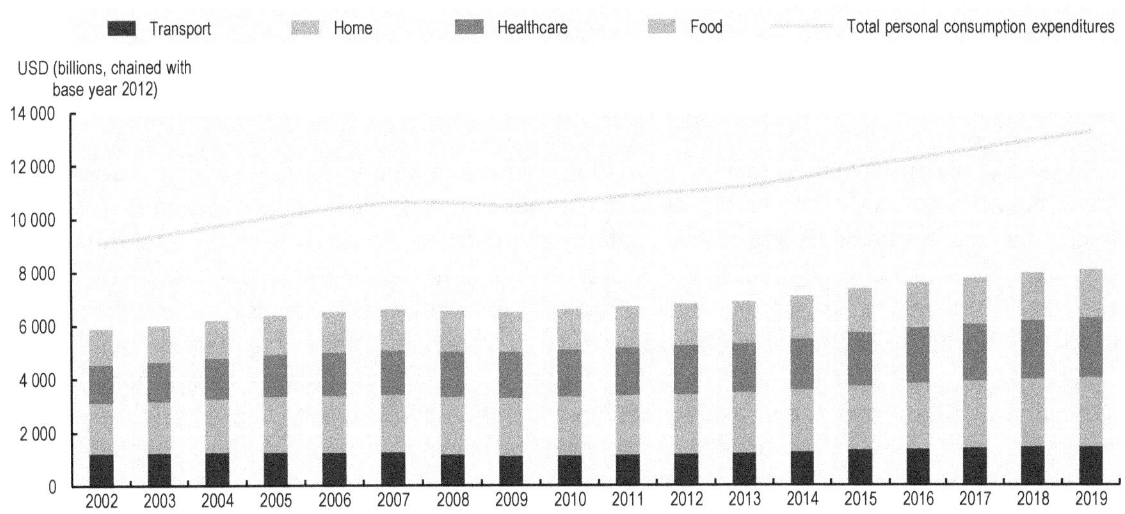

Note: Bars show the four largest groups of expenditures. Transport includes spending on motor vehicles and parts, gasoline and other energy goods, and transportation services. Home includes spending on furnishings and durable household equipment, and housing and utilities (services). Food includes spending on food and beverages purchased for off-premises consumption, and food services and accommodations.
Source: BEA (2020[26]), *GDP & Personal Income [Database]*, https://apps.bea.gov/iTable/index_nipa.cfm.

Box 1.1. Proposals for promoting affordable housing and transport in London

London's Transport Strategy includes a series of proposals intended to embed public transport in current and future developments. There are more than 600 rail and tube stations in London and the government intends to explore options for development around them. Some of the options are converting land use from low-density uses (retail, storage, parking) to high-density mixed-use development. This change should be a catalyst for the regeneration of town centres and neighbourhoods. Some of the proposals are:

The Mayor (through Transport for London, TfL) and the boroughs will:

- Seek opportunities for densification of development supported by the public transport network, in particular around public transport stations and stops; and investment in improving station environments, interchanges and local walking and cycling networks.
- Impose high expectations of developers to deliver transport solutions that will promote a shift to active, efficient and sustainable modes, reduce road congestion, improve air quality and assist in the development of attractive and healthy places.
- Restrict car parking provision within new developments, with those locations more accessible to public transport expected to be car-free. New developments should contain high levels of cycle parking and storage, and contribute to the provision of on-street cycle parking in town centres and places of high demand.
- Support growth through transport investment and planning in the Central Activities Zone (CAZ), in and around town centres, in close proximity to stations and opportunity areas. Planning framework should set mode share targets, and boroughs and stakeholders have to demonstrate how development plans will contribute to mode-shift away from car use to walking, cycling and public transport.

Source: Greater London Authority (2018[25]), *Mayor's Transport Strategy*, http://www.london.gov.uk (accessed on 15 July 2019).

One of the risks of densification is that the price of housing close to transit areas tends to rise to the point that only people who can afford to live near transit are the least likely to depend on it. City centres, especially the well-connected parts of the centres, can exclude economically vulnerable groups. One lesson from the experience of Metro Vancouver is that one additional criterion to assess housing affordability is proximity to transit. Housing affordability has been a challenge for authorities in Metro Vancouver where house prices around transit areas have increased, making the metropolitan area one of the most expensive places to live in Canada. Metro Vancouver has the highest average monthly costs for homes with a mortgage and one of the highest monthly rents in the country. Working households in the metropolitan area can spend up to 50% of their pre-tax income on housing and transportation costs. Affordable housing in prized zones is endangered, though pressure on municipalities to increase residential density near main transit lines is growing. Rents are cheaper in other areas not close to transit zones but the transport costs make them the most expensive.

Box 1.2. Metro Vancouver affordable housing strategy

Metro Vancouver's Regional Growth Strategy calls for more density near transit hubs and urban centres to reduce reliance on cars, promote neighbourhood walkability and house the one million newcomers expected by 2040. Higher density development areas are located close to SkyTrain stations within a perimeter of 400 metres. The plans consider commercial and residential areas but sometimes it is challenging for local authorities to attract new office uses due to the lack of amenities in some of the municipalities. The suburbs of some cities need to be retrofitted as they are highly car-oriented and lack public transit infrastructure. Improving the frequency of the bus service and bike lanes as part of road-widening works is seen as one possible solution to enhance accessibility.

Expanding the Frequent Transit Network (FTN), concentrating new growth and development around existing FTN corridors, is expected to help give more households an option to be less auto-dependent and reduce their transport expenditure. To meet the challenge, authorities plan to build new rapid transit lines, new line bus corridors and more frequent bus routes throughout the region. The aim is to expand the transit-oriented locations to make the transit and affordable housing connection. But partnerships and concerted efforts are necessary to make affordable housing a reality.

Source: Metro Vancouver (2017[27]), *Transit-oriented Affordable Housing Study 2017-2019*, http://www.metrovancouver.org/services/regional-planning/housing-affordability/transit-oriented/Pages/default.aspx (accessed on 25 June 2018); Metro Vancouver (2015[22]), *The Metro Vancouver Housing and Transportation Cost Burden Study - A New Way of Looking at Affordability*, http://www.metrovancouver.org/services/regional-planning/PlanningPublications/HousingAndTransportCostBurdenReport2015.pdf (accessed on 29 June 2018).

Policies that favour densification or expand the offer of affordable housing can help the spread of benefits to different socio-economic groups. The SHIFT programme adopted in Korea in 2007 is a remarkable example of how land use and social policy need to go hand in hand for transport infrastructure investment to be effective and inclusive (OECD, 2016[28]). Housing affordability in the areas that received access to public transport infrastructure was achieved by: i) allowing both low- and middle-class families to lease apartments in these areas at financially advantageous conditions; and ii) incentivising developers to build more apartments through a mix of re-zoning and higher floor-to-area ratios. Overall, relaxing height constraints around the stations of the new bus rapid transit (BRT) system in 2004 did not prevent prices for retail space and private apartments from rising but helped keep the increase in check (OECD, 2016[28]).

Inclusive transport policies can unlock growth in cities.[5] Estimates for the UK show that strengthening public transportation running between a job-rich and a job-poor area in a given city can allow for a reduction in unemployment in job-poor areas. Manning and Petrongolo (Manning and Petrongolo, 2017[29]) assess the benefits from a reduction in transport costs between Stratford in east London (the site of the 2012 Olympic Games) and central London and find that it would trigger an increase in the probability of finding a job in Stratford since more people would start looking for a job in central London.[6] The absence of inclusive policies can also be a drag for urban growth. This is the case, for example, of Aix-Marseille, France, where the expansion of the metropolitan area is held back by a social context characterised by very high inequality, which contributes to a high crime rate and therefore reduces the attractiveness of Marseille as a destination city in spite of rising labour demand (OECD, 2013[30]).

Building intermodal and integrated transport systems

Another strategy to improve the performance of the transport system as a whole in cities is the one that focuses on increasing transport intermodality. Transport intermodality refers to the integration across the networks for different transport modes available in a city. As the size of the total network expands, transport performance improves. An intermodal trip starts, for instance, in the commuting zone on public transport and ends, for instance, in the city centre, where the last mile to reach a destination is more comfortably done via cycling or micromobility. A crucial part of well-designed intermodal transport is a unique ticketing system. Intermodal transit hubs favouring the switch between transport modes can support the system. Another strategic choice that favours intermodality consists of ensuring that public transport vehicles can accommodate passengers travelling with their bike or scooter. Finally, intermodal trips can be encouraged by making walking and cycling more amenable transport mode choices for short journeys, for instance through policies making walking and cycling infrastructure safer and more comfortable to use.

Many large cities in developed and developing countries face the impact of high growth in the use of private cars for suburban commute and urban sprawl. In many instances, the majority of the population lives outside the central city of a metropolitan or functional urban area (FUA) with limited mobility options. Part of the cities' strategies to promote accessibility and the use of public transport is the creation of intermodal points and interchanges to allow at least two different modes of transport to be used in an integrated manner. Passenger transport is to a large extent intermodal public transport as people change from one mode to another for most of their journeys. Intermodal interchange points aim to provide a seamless journey to passengers using different modes of transport (Link, n.d.[31]). These terminals permit the different transport networks articulation that either serves to streamline intermodal mobility and to make easier connections with the high capacity modes. One of the best examples of an intermodal network is the city of Madrid whose intermodal interchange points facilitate change in transport mode for commuters living or working in the suburbs (Box 1.3). COVID-19 is creating the conditions for a higher increase in the use of private cars due to commuters' fear of contagion by using public transport. An online survey conducted in June 2020 on behalf of TransLink, the transport authority in the Metropolitan Vancouver Regional District, showed that over one-third of the population expected to increase their private vehicle use and another third expected to decrease their use of public transport.[7] In the Madrid metropolitan region, local authorities estimate that between 10% and 13% of residents will switch from public transport to private vehicles as a result of the health crisis.[8]

Box 1.3. Intermodal interchanges in Madrid

The city of Madrid has been working for the last two decades on the improvement of the interurban network's infrastructures and services. The creation of intermodal interchange points in strategic areas of the city aims to minimise the inevitable sensation of having to change from one mode of transport to another. The intermodal points are classified according to their infrastructure in three groups: interchange terminals (*intercambiadores*), intermodal areas and exchange points. The interchange stations have a critical role in access and dispersion of metropolitan journeys, while the intermodal areas and the rest of the exchange points supply journeys in the urban area. The interchange terminals act as the access gateways of Madrid's public transport system (suburban buses and suburban trains), optimising accessibility to the mainly urban transport modes. There are 12 principal metropolitan intermodal points in the city of Madrid of which 5 are interchange terminals managed by the regional transport authority. One in 2 trips in the entire region goes through 1 of these 12 nodes.

Source: CRTM (2016[32]), *Annual Report 2016*, http://www.crtm.es (accessed on 19 October 2018).

Car parking near transport hubs complements the intermodal interchange strategy. Car parks located near metro or train stations or big interchanges give drivers the opportunity to leave their car and continue travelling by public transport, at the same time avoiding traffic jams. For example, the public transport authority in Warsaw is constructing car parks for a Park and Ride (P+R) system. At the moment, there are 16 car parks with 4 654 parking places and a valid ticket is needed to be entitled to use them (ZTM, n.d.[33]).

Moreover, to develop and optimise public transport, the city of Warsaw plans to transform the Warsaw West railway station into a multimodal transport hub. The national rail reconstruction manager PKP PLK plans to reconstruct the station to provide direct connections to the trams and bus networks.[9] In Prague, the transport and development plans seek to achieve a more sustainable and multimodal system of transportation by connecting commuters in the surrounding municipalities with the existing railway system. For that, transport investment projects include a fourth metro line, new tramway lines and the construction of P+R facilities in the municipalities that surround Prague. However, research suggests that P+R schemes have a negative impact on real estate property value (Kahn, 2007[34]). Across US cities between 1970 and 2000, for example, home values near P+R stations fell by 2% with neighbourhoods experiencing increases in poverty but properties close to Walk & Ride stations generally saw their values increase more than 5% over 10 years (Kahn, 2007[34]). Access to Walk & Ride stations increases the supply of transit-oriented communities where people live, commute and shop while using their private car less frequently.

Integrated transport systems make travel easier and more affordable (World Bank, 2015[35]). The objective of an integrated public transport service is to achieve a high modal share for public transport with a seamless service by offering several alternatives to commuting that are competitive in terms of convenience and flexibility as well as costs (Veryard and Perkins, 2017[36]). Streamlining schedules, stops, fares and passenger information among underground services, buses and commuter rail allows passengers to use the system easily and for the service provider to cut down operational costs and boost operational revenue (World Bank, 2015[35]). However, seamless integration between all different forms of transport (bus, BRT, light rail, metro, trains as well as walking and cycling) is the main challenge in delivering competitive levels of service (Veryard and Perkins, 2017[36]). An integrated system involves modifying various parts of the network to avoid duplication. The public transport network of the cities of Madrid and Prague exemplify an integrated transport system (Box 1.4). Both cities are practically covered by all forms of public transport (available in the city) integrated into one system and present several common features:

- Physical integration, as the close proximity and ease of access at mode interchanges make it easy to use public transport.
- Systems, in particular bus and rail, should be integrated into a single network to complement each other.
- Fare integration, as in many cities, a single fare card for multiple services facilitates transfer between modes, also making payments convenient for passengers. Electronic fare payment systems allow passengers to be charged by distance or time, regardless of the number of transfers they make. Another advantage is that it allows different public transport operators to divide their revenues equally according to the distance travelled using a particular mode.
- Information integration to provide passengers with comprehensive, easy-to-understand information for travel planning. Passengers should have easy access to this information at home, work, school, stations, terminals, etc. Integrated schedules mean that all routes serving a particular stop or terminal are in operation at the same time to avoid leaving passengers stranded.
- Institutional integration to have a common institutional framework to be able to undertake land use planning, travel demand management and integrated public transport services. When there is no such a framework, co-operation and co-ordination among the different government agencies and public and private providers are key to ensure a seamless operation.

Box 1.4. Integrated public transport systems: The case of Madrid and Prague

Prague has a long tradition of using public transport and has one of the highest percentage shares for public transport use in the European Union (EU). Almost 70% of inhabitants in the city often use public transport as a mode of transport. One of the reasons that has arguably contributed to the high levels of public transport use is the development of the Prague Integrated Public Transport System (PID) where all means of transport are interconnected and co-ordinated. The PID is a public transport system that serves the entire area of Prague and two-thirds of the Central Bohemian Region, although there are plans to expand it to that entire region. The PID operates 3 metro lines, 31 tram lines, 248 bus lines, 26 railways, 1 funicular and 5 ferries. Travellers only need to purchase one ticket to use a combination of transport modes. The Prague Integrated Transport System has four basic principles:

- A unified regional transport system built around a rail transport (railways, metro and trams), and bus services linking-up residential areas to rail transport stations.
- P&R parking lots at train stops in the suburbs and beyond facilitate multimodal transport (car + public transport).
- Single ticket enables passengers to travel easier regardless of the selected way of transport and transport service provider.
- Competitive market conditions keep costs down, while coordination and cooperation are maintained.

The **Madrid** region (Comunidad Autónoma de Madrid, CAM) has an extensive and complex intermodal public transport system that consists of various modes of transport. Two major subsystems can be distinguished: i) the urban area of the city of Madrid with over 200 urban bus routes (EMT), 12 underground lines (Metro), one light rail line and 37 suburban train stations; and ii) the region's metropolitan area with over 100 urban bus routes, over 300 suburban lines, 5 metro lines, 3 light rail lines and 9 suburban railway lines. Both systems are connected by a series of large interchanges (*intercambiadores*) that surround the central area of the city of Madrid, channelling radial mobility between the capital and its metropolitan rings. The transport network provides services to all municipalities in the CAM. It has increased the number of bus lines across the city by 40%. The entire city considered, 66% of the population has a metro station in a radius of 600 metres (10 minutes' walk approximately). The Strategic Sustainable Mobility Plan of the Madrid region (SSMP) 2013-25 promotes the development of an integrated transport system based on four pillars:

- Administrative integration: This began with the creation of the *Consorcio Regional de Transportes de Madrid* (CRTM) as the unique public transport authority for the Madrid region and participating local governments.
- Fare integration: This was achieved with the introduction of the travel pass currently used for more than 70% of the transport journeys. The integration of the fare system at the regional level is the key characteristic of public transport in the Madrid region. There is a wide range of ticket options: among them, the multimodal and integrated travel card provides an unlimited number of trips during a month or a year.
- Modal integration: Refers to the complementarity of all of the different transport modes to achieve intermodality.
- Technological integration: Refers to the integration of data, formats, protocols and processes amongst operators, customers and authorities.

Source: For Prague: EC/UN-Habitat (2016[37]), *The State of European Cities 2016 - Cities Leading the Way to a Better Future*, http://dx.doi.org/10.2776/770065; IPR (2015[38]), *Do You Know Prague? The City in Maps, Graphs and Figures*, http://www.iprpraha.cz/uploads/assets/dokumenty/obecne/do_you_know_prague.pdf; ROPID (n.d.[39]), *Homepage*, http://stary.ropid.cz/info/we-introduce-pid__s219x903. For Madrid: CRTM (2013[40]), *Madrid, A World Reference - The Public Transport System in the Region of Madrid*, https://www.crtm.es/media/157716/wreference-2013nov-web.pdf (accessed on 22 October 2018); CRTM (2016[32]), *Annual Report 2016*, http://www.crtm.es (accessed on 19 October 2018); CRTM (2013[41]), *Plan Estratégico de Movilidad Sostenible de la Comunidad de Madrid 2013-2025*, http://www.crtm.es/plan-estrategico-movilidad-sostenible (accessed on 2 October 2018).

Transport integration requires clear regulations at the metropolitan level and, in their absence, strong co-operation and collaboration between the regional and local levels of government are necessary. As the experience of the Warsaw metropolitan area suggests (Box 1.5), an adequate metropolitan transport vision supported by the joint forces of the regional and local governments is necessary to achieve public transport integration. A transport authority operating at the metropolitan scale may facilitate the planning and co-ordination of infrastructure, fares and modal integration.

Box 1.5. Transport integration without regulations – The case of Warsaw

In Poland's capital Warsaw, the transport authority Zarząd Transportu Miejskiego (ZTM) manages the public transport system. The transport system consists of buses, trams and metro. However, the railway lines have shaped the urban form of the city and its suburbs since the 19th century. Until 2005, the national railway operator PKP managed the whole railway service and infrastructure of Warsaw. Regional trains operated by PKP were key for commuters in the metropolitan area. Even though more than 30 stations were located within the city of Warsaw, the number of passengers was very low due to the separate ticket tariffs and low-quality service and infrastructure. Moreover, for a long time, urban buses competed with the railways in the city and some suburban areas on parallel lines.

In 2002, the city of Warsaw government realised that railway lines in the city could be part of the urban transport system. The first step was to integrate tariffs but the first attempts to do so with PKP failed. In 2005, the region of Mazovia was given responsibility for regional trains, establishing the Mazovian Railways Company (KM) but there was no integration of regulations. Since the city of Warsaw wanted to have an influence on the railway service, it created the railway operator owned by the city (SKM) in 2005, with the objective of providing services to the entire Warsaw metropolitan area. City authorities had to buy new trains and build capacity in railway operations. SKM entered into competition with KM and competition did not meet passenger expectations. Negotiations between the city of Warsaw and the Mazovia region led to the gradual introduction of a common ticket. A passenger with a ZTM ticket can now travel on KM trains. Thanks to the tariff integration and the synergies between the regional and city operators, the city government was able to fully introduce an intermodal public transport system in the Warsaw metropolitan area consisting of buses, trams, metro and urban rails.

Despite progress, some challenges remain. For instance, Warsaw and the suburban communities compensate for the losses of KM, even though it is a regional authority dependent on public funding. More investment is needed to improve line capacity as the rail infrastructure is national and it is shared with national intercity and cargo operators. Transport integration has remained at the metropolitan level but has not expanded at the regional level. The train offer has led to new passengers using the train and vehicles have reached their maximum capacity level.

Source: Florczak, M. (2012[42]), "Integration without regulations", https://fsr.eui.eu/wp-content/uploads/121207_Florczak_Maciej.pdf (accessed on 9 August 2019).

Building an integrated transport system is a challenging task. Governments need to overcome a number of barriers that go from deficiencies in planning, resistance to change, the lack of a centralised transport authority, the influence of interest groups, the predominance of political priorities over technical ones and a weak implementation strategy. According to the OECD ITF, four key actions can be considered to design an effective integrated public transport system:

- Design interchange stations to provide secure, uncongested conditions for transfer via the shortest routes possible.
- Provide adequate bike parking areas at stations and stops.
- Integrate ticketing and information systems as well as the physical transport infrastructure.
- Establish integrated urban transport plans in consultation with stakeholders and the public (Veryard and Perkins, 2017[36]).

The experience of the city of Santiago, Chile, in building the Transantiago, reveals some of the hurdles authorities need to overcome to organise and implement an integrated public transport system (Box 1.6). The Transantiago is one of the most expensive and ambitious transport projects in the country's history but, despite the USD 10 billion investment since the start of the development process in 2007, citizens do not consider it delivers the service at the expected quality levels. One of the most important lessons from the implementation of the Transantiago is that when the government wants to change a transport system, it should do it gradually, phasing the scheme in several stages, allowing for adjustments as problems arise and in consultation with citizens.

Box 1.6. Chile's capital mobility network: Transantiago

The reorganisation of the Transantiago bus network in Chile's capital Santiago is one of the largest policy experiments ever conducted in the country and is a precedent for improving public transport provision (OECD, 2017[43]). Until 2007, Santiago, had a public transport system that covered the entire territory of the metropolitan area (2 000 km^2), which included the 36 communes, and offered service to 6 million inhabitants. However, the public transport system had some deficiencies that made it inefficient and ineffective such as: low occupancy rate of buses; very poor frequency in low demand periods, producing high congestion and pollution; an overlap of services on main avenues; frequent on-the-street competition for passengers; poor travel conditions for students; many micro-owners (owners of 1 or 2 buses) but strong owners unions; and poor working conditions for drivers with salaries commensurate with the number of tickets sold.

In 2007, Chilean authorities implemented a transport reform programme to modernise the public transport system in the metropolitan area of Santiago. The Transantiago project aimed at encouraging the use of public transport, improving the quality of service by eliminating on-the-street competition and replacing the existing bus fleet, improving air quality and reducing travel time.

The project had a trunk and feeder structure which intended to increase the use of the metro and avoid overlap of services. The number of buses was reduced from 10 000 to only 5 000 (to eliminate congestion). The project included an integrated fare system with the use of a smart card. To allow operators from the old system to continue working in the new one, bus owners were integrated into bigger companies. This made the Transantiago a privately operated system to minimise the risk of strikes and city paralysis. State-operated services had a poor reputation in the country and it was thought that a private system would provide better service and bring the experience of world-class operators.

However, as soon as the new system started operations, it faced a number of obstacles. There were design deficiencies that limited the efficiency of the new system. For instance, residents were not familiar with the trunk and feeder structure; the required bus fleet size was underestimated leading to insufficient coverage and lack of adjustment flexibility; payment to bus operators was based on referential demand and there was therefore no incentive to move buses; the design of the system was based on an outdated origin/destination survey (2002); and there was no focus on service quality. There were also implementation problems due to the rush to implement the new system even before basic conditions were met. For instance, most dedicated corridors for the buses were not built, the fleet control software was not operational, the information systems for users was not ready and the entire system was changed in a single day (big bang approach) as there was no transition period. The metro was overcrowded as it passed from 1.3 million users to 2.2 million. There was a financial deficit as the government froze fares, which had to be financed through subsidies.

In 2010-12, the government introduced changes to the system which included the possibility to modify contracts, the abandonment of the trunk and feeder structure, changes in the incentive system to operators from kilometres run to effective passenger transportation, fare increases and a new law that secures public funds.

In 2019, the government changed the Transantiago to a new system called Red Metropolitana de Movilidad (RED) seeking to increase the service standards and the modernisation of the procurement model of transport services. RED currently includes buses, metro and MetroTren services as part of the integrated transport system. Payments are made through a unique transport card. Different bus companies form part of the RED (i.e. Buses VULE; Subus Chile, Express de Santiago UNO, MetBus, RedBus Urbano, and Servicio de Transporte de Personas) which provide bus services in the Santiago metropolitan area and, in that way, avoid the "too big to fail" problem. Currently, Transatiago's fleet is less polluting, less accident-prone and more accessible than the previous system but some challenges remain. The system seems to be rather rigid leading to higher journey times for some passengers. Plans to improve safety and adapt routes to changing patterns of demand in a growing city seem to be at an advanced stage.

Source: Prepared based on the presentation given by Chile's Ambassador to the OECD, Felipe Morandé, to the International Transport Forum on 5 September 2019 and OECD (2017[43]), *Gaps and Governance Standards of Public Infrastructure in Chile: Infrastructure Governance Review*, https://doi.org/10.1787/9789264278875-en. For further information, see http://www.red.cl/.

Encouraging active and micromobility

A successful public transport system encourages active mobility and provides a sense of safety

Promoting and facilitating active mobility is becoming part of new developments in cities around the world. Active mobility had long been neglected in cities as the focus was on facilitating car usage. However, active mobility is gaining importance, in particular over short distances in urban and suburban areas, as well as intermodal mobility. In the aftermath of COVID-19, active mobility is regarded as the response to the new mobility needs of urban residents. Indeed, in cities across the world, public transport usage has fallen with an increasing number of people walking or riding bicycles to avoid crowded mass transits and follow health advice for physical activity and distancing. Cities like Bogotá, Brussels, Geneva, London, Mexico City, Milan and Paris are investing in extra bike lanes, some of which are temporal to respond to the emergency but others are permanent. Investing in pedestrians and cyclists, according to the United Nations (UN), can save lives, help protect the environment and support poverty reduction.[10] London's experience shows that investing in cycling can produce economic benefits as making cycling safer and easier in business districts helps to attract and retain the employees companies need to succeed (Transport for London, 2018[44]). In Spain, the use of bicycles increased by 260% in May 2020 as a result of the pandemic.[11] In the city of Madrid, there has been an increase in the use of individual mobility devices (i.e. walking, bicycles, scooters, etc). These devices are considered adequate to cover short distances and a way to avoid contagion. The transport authority in the Madrid region has authorised private providers to expand their fleets of electric bikes to up to 4 800 units more during the summer 2020 period. If the demand is met, the offer of electric bikes could reach 9 600 units. BiciMAD, Madrid's bike-sharing system, already has 2 496 units operating and is being expanded as well. Thus, authorities expect that the total number of bicycles available to the capital residents will be three times higher than in 2019.[12] However, for public transport operators, this means a reduction in the number of possible passengers and revenue.

Active mobility has underutilised the potential of green urban transport. Active mobility does not generate motorised traffic and encourages mode shift away from private cars leading to reduced emissions and less noise. Cycling as a transport mode can be a substitute for public transport, especially over short distances. In Copenhagen, 36% of the trips to work or school are made by cycling equalling to 0 tonnes of CO_2 emissions and the city aims to be CO_2-neutral by 2025 (City of Copenhagen, 2011[45]). Thanks to their substitutability, cycling is especially appealing in cities that are reaching saturation of their local public transport network, such as the city centre of Paris. However, cycling and public transport can also be complementary. First, cycling can significantly expand the catchment area of rail stations (ITF, 2018[46]). Second, bicycle-sharing systems in the city centre of cities allow commuters to bridge the "last mile" between public transport stops and their final destinations. Incentivising cycling entails deploying the physical infrastructure needed for riders to feel comfortable using bikes, such as having dedicated bike lanes, dedicated parking lots, especially near rail stations, and bike-accessible trains.

Box 1.7. Defining active mobility and micromobility

Active mobility and micromobility are two closely related concepts that may even be used as equivalents but there are some differences. Active mobility is a generic term to identify any form of human-powered transportation such as walking, cycling, skating, kick scooters, etc. Micromobility includes the use of exclusively human-powered vehicles, such as bicycles, skates, skateboards and kick scooters (ITF, 2020[47]). It refers to personal transportation using devices and vehicles weighing up to 350 kg and whose power supply, if any, is gradually reduced and cut off at a given speed limit which is no higher than 45 km/h. Micromobility can include the model of shared usage. There is no rigid separation between micro and shared mobility: micromobility indeed often comes in the form of shared mobility, so long as the devices and vehicles are third-party-owned and accessible on demand by travellers. In recent years, the growing use of electric light vehicles such as e-bikes and e-scooter has given rise to the term electric micromobility or e-micromobility.

Source: ITF (2020[47]), *Safe Micromobility*, https://www.itf-oecd.org/sites/default/files/docs/safe-micromobility_1.pdf (accessed on 21 September 2020).

Cycling and walking are the fastest and least expensive modes for door-to-door travel for many short-distance trips. Walking and cycling are considered as the investment areas that can contribute the most to achieving cities' strategic goals such as reducing congestion and improving public and environmental health, at the lowest net cost. According to the city of Copenhagen, taking a bicycle results in a net profit for society of DKK 3.65 (USD 0.58) while taking a car results in a net loss for society of DKK 6.59 (USD 1.04) (City of Copenhagen, 2011[45]). Investment in cycling infrastructure seems also to produce value for money. The Dutch government spends EUR 30 (USD 35) per annum per person on bike infrastructure – 15 times the amount spent in England – which represents 3% of the government's transport and traffic budget. The results have been lower carbon emissions and high health levels (Hawkins Kreps, 2018[48]). Cycling is also a more inclusive way of travelling, as it is more affordable than driving. To unlock cycling's potential, cities are investing in traffic-protected bikeways that provide the safety and comfort needed. For instance, London is investing in building a cycle network with major new routes across the city and creating local routes and neighbourhood schemes. Moreover, that transport authority has put into service a new Cycling Infrastructure Database (CID) available to everyone. The CID provides services such as: tailored journey planning, cycle parking mapping, and informing TfL and borough plans (Transport for London, 2018[44]). Cycling in London has more than doubled since 2000: on average, cycling levels rose by 5.8% between 2000 and 2017 and there was an overall 24% increase between 2012 and 2017 (Transport for London, 2018[44]). London's transport strategy's central aim is for 80% of all trips in London to be made on foot, by cycle or using public transport by 2041, compared to 63% in 2015 (Greater London Authority, 2018[25]).

To encourage active mobility, cities are improving sidewalks, street crossings and other walking infrastructure. This includes removing barriers and expand walking access to transit to make more efficient and safer use of streets for short journeys. COVID-19 has created the momentum for cities to invest in walking and cycling infrastructure as part of their emergency infrastructure projects. However, it is important that cities link emergency infrastructure to long-term urban accessibility objectives by investing in building infrastructure now that they want to keep for the future (ITF, 2020[49]). Providing more and better services to make public transport the best option for longer ones is a complementary action. A shift from car use to more space-efficient means of transport is a long-term solution to congestion and contributes to properly functioning cities. According to the experience of London, a successful public transport system is one that encourages walking and cycling (Greater London Authority, 2018[25]). New developments are required to discourage the use of private cars through the provision of limited and costly car parking services or the reduction of the "implicit" subsidies that encourage the use of private cars (e.g. lower fuel prices, support for parking and fuel from the employers). Other measures include enabling shared use services models and developing safety standards for new services entering the market and reviewing existing regulatory frameworks. New York City's strategic plan aims to allocate more street space to walking, biking and buses as they move the greatest number of people while using the least amount of street capacity. For that, the Department of Transportation is enhancing and expanding the 1 000-mile (1 600 km) bike network, increasing the bike parking opportunities and expanding the bike-sharing programme to the 5 boroughs (NYC Department of Transportation, 2016[17]).

Not all cities have the right infrastructure and urban form for encouraging cycling and walking and, like in many Eastern EU cities, their mode share is generally low. In the Romanian cities of Sibiu and Timişoara accessibility by walking is rather limited due to the low priority for pedestrians in the organisation of public spaces. The problem is worst in residential areas due to narrow or absent sidewalks or stairways, obstacles built or located on sidewalks, heavily damaged surfaces and the lack of adequate connecting ramps with walkways and pedestrian crossings. The lack of sidewalks is a major and frequently encountered problem in suburban areas of both cities. In the Metro Vancouver Regional District, some neighbourhoods of the municipalities of New Westminster and Surrey, mainly rural ones, do not have walking infrastructure. In many places in the region, poor walking connectivity to the FTN and rapid transit stations is deterring ridership and making those investments less effective than they could otherwise be. Thus, the transport authority, TransLink, is working with the different municipalities to share the costs of pedestrian facility upgrades within walking distance of frequent transit stops, stations and exchanges. In Athens, walking and cycling as mobility options are relatively underdeveloped as there are no dedicated cycling lanes in central areas and cycling is considered to be difficult and risky given the other vehicles' driving behaviour (OECD, 2015[50]).

However, some cities are making progress in the promotion of active mobility. In Mexico City, the ECOBICI programme has achieved significant success in increasing bicycle use by residents in the entire metropolitan area. In 2015, 45% of trips with ECOBICI were for commuting. Along with the ECOBICI system, other programmes have been introduced in Mexico City to encourage bicycle use such as the conversion of several streets and avenues to bicycle and pedestrian use on Sunday mornings. The programme Travel by Bike (*Muévete en Bici*), implemented in 2007 started with 10 km of road space being closed to motorised traffic every Sunday morning; by 2012, the road space was expanded to 24 km (OECD, 2015[51]).

Micromobility and e-micromobility as an alternative to public transport

Cities are using micromobility to encourage active mobility, in particular light electric devices. Micromobility has surged in recent years, particularly in the city centre of large cities. Sydney's transport strategy considers that assisted mobility devices, such as e-bikes and motorised scooters, have the potential to move people out of single-occupant cars for the first mile and last mile of trips, freeing up capacity on the roads for people who need to travel further. The advantage of these devices is that they are faster and require less physical effort than walking and cycling. Lisbon, for instance, which was awarded the title of European Green Capital in 2020, deployed a large fleet of electrical bikes to help users overcome the difficulties associated with travelling by bike in a hilly city.

In recent years, the use of electric micromobility (e-micromobility) devices has increased across the world. The number of e-bike shares systems with at least 100 e-bikes grew from 1 in 2013 to 18 in 2019, and the total of e-bikeshare bicycles passed from 2 500 in 2013 to more than 40 000 in 2019 (Yanocha, 2019[52]). In the US, in 2018, people took 84 million trips on shared micromobility, more than double the number of trips taken in 2017.[13] In fact, in 2018, e-scooters overtook bikes as the preferred vehicle for dockless vendors in the US with 85 000 e-scooters available for public use in 100 US cities. In China, the annual e-bike sales passed from just over 20 million units in 2009 to over 35 million in 2018 (Yanocha, 2019[52]).

The key advantages of micromobility are its flexibility and low cost. Micromobility devices have a lower operating cost than owning and operating private cars and are even further reduced when sharing schemes are available. According to the experience of Western Australia, the use of e-bikes has the potential to make people leave their cars at home. The use of e-bikes helped decrease commuting by car from 61% to 32% for trips as a driver or passenger (NSW Government, 2018, p. 62[53]). Electric mobility devices can also provide widespread access to nearby destinations quickly, minimise harm to the environment, promote equity and affordability, maximise resource efficiency, maintain safety and contribute to a healthy lifestyle. E-bike sharing at interchanges has the potential to increase the use of public transport as e-bikes can better connect people to the mass transit network.

Promoting electric mobility requires care. Cities need to consider a number of issues that may go wrong when making investments (Yanocha, 2019[52]). For instance, there could be a high demand for public parking and charging infrastructure that local governments will have to consider and install. The efficiency of the system could be damaged if there is an oversupply and indiscriminately parked devices clutter the streets. If the charging systems for shared devices are inefficient, it could lead to an increase of energy use. Health outcomes may be compromised if electric micromobility replaces walking and pedal cycling trips. Regarding safety, without proper infrastructure, the number of accidents and crashes may increase. There are also equity and affordability concerns as availability may be limited to higher-income neighbourhoods or only to those who possess a smartphone or credit card, and their use could be too expensive for low-income groups without fare integration with transit (shared systems). Moreover, elderly and disabled people may not be conformable or feel safe in using those devices.

How can cities promote micromobility?

With new technological developments and the introduction of new types of electric micromobility devices cities need a clearer classification. The goal is to bring clarity on what constitutes an electric micromobility device as their use and where they can be used will depend on it. Cities could classify e-bikes and scooters as non-motor vehicles and clearly define the maximum speed for low (25 km/h) and moderate (top speed 45 km/h) speed electric devices. It is also important that cities define the infrastructure that electric devices are permitted to use to improve safety and order in the streets. For instance, the city of Madrid is becoming a lab for an innovative mobility regulation. Due to the transformation of means of transport over the last five to ten years, authorities have enacted a regulation that addresses the circulation of alternative means of transport. The approach to regulate this issue has been to make a clear distinction for a different type of new vehicles:

- Vehicles for urban mobility (electric kickboards, Segways, etc.): The local regulation uses the classification of the type of motor vehicles (A, B, C0, C1 y C2) established by the national General Traffic Directorate through the Norm 16/V-124. It then establishes that this type of vehicle has to circulate either on roads (where maximum speed is 30 km/h) or bicycle lanes. It also regulates the equipment (lights, braking device, whistle, etc.) that these vehicles have to incorporate to circulate legally.
- Rollerblades and kickboards, or similar vehicles, with no motor: Will be able to circulate on sidewalks at a maximum speed of 5 km/h and on all types of bicycle lane.
- Skateboards: Follow a similar regulation to rollerblades and kickboards, but their circulation will be forbidden on sidewalks or bicycle lanes that are too steep. This is to ensure safety since this kind of device has no brakes. For sports purposes, users will have to go to the specific authorised areas.

Cities can design safe and inclusive on-street infrastructure, enforce the safe use of cycling infrastructure, and offer public safe-riding courses. To manage and monitor the functioning of the electric micromobility systems, cities need to integrate small electric modes into citywide strategies and plans, and collect data for analysis and enforcement (Yanocha, 2019[52]).

Active mobility requires political commitment and long-term investments

Active mobility infrastructure requires political support. Making cycling a priority in urban accessibility requires strong political conviction and planning. Cities like Copenhagen and London have even issued cycling strategic plans supported by their local authorities. Promoting active mobility is not just an issue for the departments of transport, it is widespread across most policy fields. Thus, broad commitment and co-ordination from various policy departments make it easier to integrate active mobility and micromobility into long-term political goals on environment, well-being and economic development.

Active mobility initiatives require a steady and reliable financial flow. Countries and cities are spending more on walking and cycling infrastructure. For example, the Netherlands plans to invest EUR 552 million on bicycle infrastructure with the aim of getting an additional 200 000 Dutch people on bicycles (Reid, 2018[54]). A well-planned and consistently financed package for infrastructure and regulation is essential to promoting active mobility. One key aspect is that active mobility infrastructure has to compete with other modes of transport budget investments priorities even if they are relatively low cost. Thus, cycling measures need to be planned holistically and at the same time as other urban improvements like housing and parks. Active mobility infrastructure investments require ongoing sustainable funding to retrofit, build, maintain, improve, promote and expand the network. However, most cities do not begin with long-term funding. Research suggests that there are four stages for funding cycling infrastructure in a more sustainable way in the long term (Box 1.8).

Box 1.8. Overcoming challenges for funding cycling infrastructure

Stage one: Demonstration projects. Cities without a cycling culture and infrastructure need to start somewhere to create momentum. Trial projects can get over the inertia and fear of change by establishing initial success. These projects are usually lower-cost and build confidence and support for the higher-price project. Funding can come from outside the private sector, for example form agencies interested in health, energy and environment benefits.

Stage two: Policy-driven funding. After the trial period, the next stage is to design a sustainable programme; this involves creating a master plan and adopting other policies to modify existing transport plans so as to make cycling part of all transport plans. Cycling infrastructure would then be built as a component of larger infrastructure projects.

Stage three: Routine funding. Timely implementation of a cycling network requires independent retrofit projects prioritised in a cycling master plan. Most cycling programmes have an annual budget amount that is supplemented by special project funds, often from regional and national programmes. Successful projects can be the basis for budget support from champions of the bicycle programme across the board. Measurable progress can also help ensure continued and increased funding. Funding from outside the transport sector also needs to be considered, for example from local development programmes.

Stage four: Accelerated success. Once the bicycle programme has been funded, the next stage is to maintain a plateau level of funding. It is sometimes vision and competition with other cities, regions and even countries that fuel big budgets. Pointing the virtues of other cities' cycling network can positively influence decision-makers.

Source: CiViTAS (2013[55]), *Enabling Cycling Cities: Ingredients for Success*, http://www.pas-port.info/cycling (accessed on 3 June 2020).

Going smart, shared, autonomous and electric

In 2017, transport, the second largest sector in terms of CO_2 emissions, accounted for 24% of total carbon emissions from fuel combustion (IEA, 2019[56]). Moreover, over the past 50 years, CO_2 emissions from the transport sector have grown faster than any other sector (OECD, 2019[57]). CO_2 emissions from the transport sector have grown at an annual rate of 2% points during 2000-17. CO_2 emissions from road passenger transport – of which urban transport made up 53% in 2015 (ITF, 2017[58]) – have grown at an annual rate of 2.4%, hence almost at a half percentage point higher rate (IEA, 2019[56]). Urban transport is undergoing a rapid and profound change that puts it at the forefront of the transition towards a climate-neutral economy.

Urban transport systems need to provide different mobility alternatives to commuters if it is to play a fundamental role in reducing air pollution. Local policymakers trying to bring down car usage in their cities and promoting alternative means of transport need to ensure that their public transport systems are sufficiently accessible. Without a sufficiently accessible public transport system, price-based instruments, such as carbon taxes or congestion charges, can exacerbate inequalities in spite of making the economy as a whole better-off. The negative distributional impact of such policies materialises when individuals being taxed do not have alternative means of transport to turn to. The negative impact can be offset, for example, by reinvesting the revenues generated from the tax into public transport improvements (Anable and Goodwin, 2018[59]). Carbon taxes can also present an efficiency-equity trade-off. Raising carbon taxes without complementary redistributive measures can in fact exacerbate the rural-urban divide since people living outside of urban areas spend far more on fuel than urban residents. The negative distributional impact can be offset by means of a redistributive policy from urban to rural areas, or avoided altogether by means of differential taxation of car usage, depending on whether it takes place in rural or urban areas.[14]

Shared mobility has boomed in recent years, especially in an urban context. A shared mobility service is characterised by an optimised shared-vehicle fleet system that provides on-demand transport and is typically enabled by an application-based digital platform (ITF, 2019[60]). Car (or motorcycle) sharing is a type of shared mobility and typically refers to the service through which private individuals can rent a vehicle owned by a third party – whether a company or another private individual – for a short duration and typically in an urban context.[15] In many cities, the car-sharing market is quite competitive and populated by a high number of companies, each owning their fleet of cars and/or motorcycles that customers can easily locate and rent through the respective applications. The proliferation of providers has led in certain countries and cities to the entry into the market of an intermediary integrating the information on various providers into a single application (e.g. Urbi). The car-sharing market keeps expanding and its definitions being redrawn. While the "car-to-go" formula is so far the most widely adopted, there are several car-sharing alternatives that are being developed. For instance, GaiaGo is an application that makes it easier for households living in the same condominium to share a car by allowing for efficient co-ordination of personal trips.

According to the projections elaborated by the ITF, shared mobility could halve the number of vehicle-kilometres travelled in urban areas if widely adopted. This could lead to a 30% decrease in CO_2 emissions from urban transport by 2050 relative to projections based on current ambitions. Shared mobility was only responsible for 1.5% of worldwide urban passenger-kilometres in 2015 but, by 2050, it is likely to cover more than one-fifth of urban trips (ITF, 2019[60]).

Electric vehicles (EVs) can also accelerate the transition towards a climate-neutral economy, especially if renewable energy is used to power them (ITF, 2018[61]). The uptake of EVs correlates very strongly with the extent of subsidies or tax breaks put in place in countries and cities to make EV prices more competitive. For instance, Norway managed to get the EV sales share to rise from 20% to 32% within just 1 year between 2017 and 2018 thanks to their effective system of subsidies and tax breaks (BMU, 2018[62]).[16]

While important, price incentives are not sufficient. McKinsey research shows that drivers who choose EVs tend to be high-income, have tertiary degrees and generally be more sensitive to environmental issues (McKinsey & Company, 2014[63]). Hence, both national and local policies need to devote greater efforts towards increasing the sensitivity to environmental issues of the general public. Moreover, the price of EVs is expected to remain higher than internal combustion engine ones well beyond 2050 (ITF, 2018[61]). Governments should therefore consider substantially scaling up their investment efforts in green technologies if the price gap is to close in a relatively short period.[17]

Local government can also incentivise the uptake of EVs by, for instance, excluding EVs from local congestion charges. A study on the London congestion charge finds that that greater proximity to the charge zone is positively associated with hybrid and EV registrations, implying that this policy has been effective at promoting the adoption of low emission vehicles (Morton, Lovelace and Anable, 2017[64]).

Local authorities can help the diffusion of EVs by ensuring the widespread presence of charging stations. The cost of a two-plug charging station is about EUR 2 000 (McKinsey & Company, 2014[63]). Since this can be a too high investment for many individuals, local authorities can intervene and provide the charging infrastructure. Alternatively, they can incentivise employers and owners of other popular destinations where car owners typically park their cars (e.g. shopping malls) to do so. Providing the incentives for the network of private charging stations to grow can effectively compensate for the limits associated with charging stations located in public parking areas. In some neighbourhoods, car owners might indeed park their cars predominantly in privately-owned spaces, such as garages, therefore limiting the utilisation of government-provided charging stations located in public parking areas.

Finally, cities must aim at minimising the CO_2 footprint of all means of transport, including shared ones. Many cities are moving towards electrification of their public transport system. For example, in London, as of 2018, any new public buses must be hybrid, electric or hydrogen, in line with the current administration goal of making London a carbon-free city by 2050 (Greater London Authority, 2018[25]).

Autonomous vehicles have the potential to enhance accessibility

The adoption of autonomous vehicles (AVs) – driverless cars – does not need to be in contrast with environmental goals. On the contrary, AVs have the potential to accelerate the transition towards a climate-neutral economy. It would be indeed more convenient for users to switch to a shared or green mobility solution if alongside it they could use the time saved on driving to do other more fulfilling tasks. Local and national policymakers need to take a more proactive stance in providing private actors the right incentives for these innovations to accelerate the transition towards a climate-neutral economy.

AVs are the next game-changer in urban mobility. They have the potential to provide citizens with more flexible travel options, greater safety and faster journeys. To enhance their effectiveness, these vehicles are designed to provide shared services to help reduce congestion and extend the catchment area of the public transport network. They will also improve the mobility of people who cannot drive today, for example because of disabilities or age. While self-driving cars have the potential to improve many aspects of daily life, they could also create a series of undesired consequences if regulation does not keep pace (OECD, 2019[65]). The benefits depend on the costs and rate of take-up, the ownership models and the number of customers. But there are risks involved as well, such as the increase in traffic volumes, an increase in vehicle-kilometres travelled and higher greenhouse gas (GHG) emissions. Therefore, governments need to explore and identify appropriate policy and regulatory mechanisms to ensure that driverless cars support their transport and accessibility strategies. For example, governments may adapt the regulatory framework to enable innovation without hindering other societal outcomes such as equity and safety. However, they do not necessarily need to regulate all outcomes as private sector actions may be guided by tools others than regulation, such as voluntary agreements. Moreover, governments do not need to regulate everything that is new but may remove existing regulation where it is no longer warranted or adapt it. Regulations should be iterative and flexible in order to account for many unknowns around the uptake of automated vehicles and other transport technologies and services (ITF/OECD, 2020[66])

Box 1.9. Smart shuttle trial – Sydney Olympic Park

The New South Wales government in partnership with HMI Technologies, IAG, NRMA and the Sydney Olympic Park Authority conducted a trial of an autonomous shuttle bus. This pilot exercise started in August 2017 and was the first, precinct-based trial of an automated shuttle in the country. The trial focused on testing automated vehicle technology and presented a unique opportunity to develop a research platform that improves citizens' mobility. The trial aimed to understand what supporting technology and infrastructures were needed to operate an automated shuttle in this environment, how it interacted with other precinct users such as pedestrians, cyclists, etc., and how it integrateed with the broader transport network. This trial provided some light regarding passengers' responses to this type of vehicle and the services it can enable, such as on-demand transport at off-peak times.

Source: NSW Government (2018[53]), *Future Transport Strategy 2056*, https://future.transport.nsw.gov.au/sites/default/files/media/documents/2018/Future_Transport_2056_Strategy.pdf.

At the time of writing this report, only cars that can drive autonomously under certain circumstances are available on the market. While the technology underlying fully automated vehicles is far from ready for commercialisation today, most experts expect AVs to become available at some point during the next decade. Fully automated vehicles will probably not become available everywhere at the same time. Most likely, cities or countries with advantageous climate conditions (e.g. no snow and little rain), orderly traffic and a favourable regulatory environment will see an earlier introduction than other places. Such a staggered introduction offers policymakers two advantages. First, the timeline for the introduction of self-driving cars becomes more predictable once a large-scale rollout begins in some countries. Second, policymakers in most countries will be able to learn from the experience of the early adopters and can adjust their policies accordingly to deal with any undesired consequences (OECD, 2019[65]).

In the absence of a more decisive policy direction, the net social benefits of automated vehicles are uncertain. The adoption of AVs entails both private benefits and social costs. On one hand, AVs improve the quality of life of commuters by allowing them to redirect their energy away from driving and towards other tasks, such as working, reading or sleeping during the commute to and from work. On the other hand, precisely because commuting becomes more pleasant, people may decide to switch from public transport to private car ridership and live much further away from cities than they do at present in order to live in larger homes or be surrounded by more green space, thus potentially leading to a resurgence of suburbanisation. Better planning at the metropolitan level is necessary to prevent uncontrolled suburbanisation (OECD, 2019[65]).

There is substantial disagreement among experts concerning the consequences of AVs on private car ridership. A survey run by the ITF asked a number of experts whether they believed that AV technology would increase car usage or not. The majority (54%) answered that it would, since: i) by reducing the time spent in traffic or looking for parking, it would make car ridership a relatively more attractive alternative and induce a switch from other transport modes; ii) it would make car ridership accessible to those that are too young or too old to drive (ITF, 2018[61]). Thirty percent replied that car usage would go down because of the savings in the estimated time required to complete a ride and thanks to the combination of AVs with car-sharing solutions. The remaining 16% agreed that AVs would not significantly affect car ridership.

To understand how AV adoption would change commuter behaviour and gauge the extent of associated benefits, it is important to consider the consequences it would have for different types of journeys. Between 1976 and 2010, average daily travel time for residents of the French île-de-France region has increased from 76 minutes per day to 92 in spite of the substantial improvements in the transport network (IAU, 2016[67]). The rise in travel time dedicated to leisure-related trips is responsible for this increase. Several factors may be behind the rise in travel time dedicated to leisure-related journeys: the decline in hours worked, demographic change, more entertainment opportunities. Since most entertainment opportunities tend to be located in the amenities-rich city centre of cities, the increasing demand for leisure-related trips is an attraction force that pulls housing demand towards the city centre, effectively countering any tendency towards urban sprawl. It is possible that AVs may reduce user cost especially for this type of trip, since user cost for job-related trips is already fairly low thanks to public transport. In this case, some people would not mind living further out in the commuting zone since they could more easily access leisure opportunities located in the city centre. If this were the case, the social cost of AV adoption in terms of increased urban sprawl would certainly be high and might not offset the private benefit experienced by commuters.

Smart mobility projects can enhance accessibility

Smart mobility is one of the key components of smart city policies. It builds on the concept of intelligent transport systems (ITS), which focuses on intermeshing digital technologies among devices, vehicles and infrastructure for better traffic management. Smart mobility also includes communicative assets (vehicles, infrastructure and other objects), mobility data platforms and shared mobility services. All these component together have the potential to improve mobility and accessibility outcomes and reduce the negative externalities related to transport activity (ITF/OECD, 2020[66]). Indeed, mobility is increasingly technology-led. Data sharing and smartphone applications are enabling more flexible approaches to matching citizens' transport demand with transport services. Over the last decade, mobile technology is improving the customer interface by providing a single platform for trip planning, payment and travel information. Ridesharing services exemplify how technology – mainly through advances in Global Positioning System (GPS) navigation devices – smartphones and networks can co-ordinate drivers, customers and payment systems. "Smart mobility promises a virtuous cycle of technological innovation, new services, and improved outcomes for people ... but it does not guarantee these" (ITF/OECD, 2020, p. 6[66]). Realising the benefits of smart mobility requires addressing some challenges such as re-bound effects that could generate additional travel, which may erode many potential benefits, and smart mobility that could improve bit also diminish equity outcomes; there are also concerns about the privacy impacts of smart mobility data, and traditional regulatory tools and processes, which may not be adapted to new technologies and services (ITF/OECD, 2020[66]).

Automated metro systems are becoming more common around the world. Users already use applications to receive information in real-time and plan their journeys. They can also use electronic ticketing via transport cards (i.e. Navigo card in Paris, Oyster card in London, Opal card in Sydney, Compass card in Vancouver, Isar card in Munich or Octopus card in Hong Kong). These cards, by providing an integrated tariff system, ensure seamless journeys across transport modes in the areas covered.

Smart mobility projects create opportunities to improve the capacity of the existing network and enhance accessibility at the same time. Their advantage is that they may lead to more cost-effective transport service delivery by making the most of the existing infrastructure. Cities need to be prepared to ensure the safe and effective adoption of ITS, ensuring they contribute to the city's overall vision of transport and accessibility. Some of the actions national and local governments may need to explore to be better prepared to adapt the new technology to meet the cities' strategic goals are: enabling new and upgraded physical infrastructure and digital assets to support new technologies; identifying road infrastructure that supports automated vehicles; and implementing intelligent traffic management methods.

Cities are experimenting Mobility as a Service (MaaS) applications that allow citizens access to mobility services in a simple, easy-to-understand way. MaaS is a service model that enables users to plan and pay for their journeys using a range of services via a single customer interface, such as a mobile application. Users can hop on any bus, train, tram, metro, bicycle, taxi, ferry, car-share, rental car, etc. for a single monthly fee, for instance, with trip routing suggestions based on users' specific, prioritised criteria (i.e. lowest cost, shortest travel time, space for large items, wheelchair accessibility, lowest carbon footprint). MaaS relies on sharing real-time information across different transport providers to help users optimise their journeys through a single MaaS platform. Finland's capital Helsinki is currently experimenting with this service model and the first results show a 25% increase in the use of public transport (Rodriguez, 2017[68]). In the city of Turku, Finland, the implementation of a MaaS platform has led to an increase in 20% in the number of public transport users with people claiming to have sold their family's second car. Ninety-eight percent of customers considered that the introduction of the platform, known as Föli, has increased the attractiveness of public transport in their everyday life. MaaS has also reduced commuting by private car between municipalities, as 9% of customers on regional lines are completely new public transport users and 42% had the opportunity to use their car but preferred public transport instead (Taskinen et al., 2016[69]).

All technological and service developments have important implications for the government's role in the transport domain. Governments increasingly assume the role of enabler of the use of new technology. They do this through regulation, service provision and collaboration with the private sector and researchers. The future role of government will be mainly to focus on setting network and customer outcomes and ensure policy and regulatory frameworks are in place to support new service models. City governments will need to review regulations governing road, rail and bus operations to provide arrangements that can pre-empt or respond quickly to market disruptions.

Making transport and accessibility gender-sensitive

Travel by public transport is highly gendered. Nowadays, women travel widely to access employment, education, leisure, etc. However, transport today is neither planned nor designed to be gender-sensitive (Allen, 2019[70]). It is usually women who have to take care of domestic chores, children, the elderly and sick, while they also participate in productive activities; this dictates their travel patterns and behaviours, and they tend to travel more if they have a family. The time lost in travelling is therefore far more penalising for women. There are significant differences between men and women regarding the mode of transport they use. In Europe, fewer women than men own or use a car. For example, in Sweden, 70% of the cars are owned by men. In France, 60% of men living outside the Paris region travel by car (Duchène, 2011[71]). In the city of Gothenburg, only 34% of women travel by car (City of Gothenburg, 2014[72]). In Mexico City, men conduct 26% of their trips by car while women only 18% (SEMOVI, 2019[73]). However, the situation is beginning to change. In the US, the number of women with driving licenses is overtaking that of men; 2.6 million more women are licenced to drive than men.[18] Canada is close to having more women with a driving license (49.95%) (Singh, 2014[74]). In the UK, the number of driving licence applications is increasing by 2.5% more for women than for men (Singh, 2014[74]).

Women tend to make more of their trips on foot than men. In Mexico City, women make 33% of the trips on foot whereas men only 19.5% (SEMOVI, 2019[73]). In Malmö, women conduct 17% of their trips by walking whereas men only 12% (City of Malmö, 2016[24]). In African countries, walking is the most commonly used mode of transport by women (57% in Bamako, 69% in Niamey, and 73% in Dakar) and the problem is particularly acute in rural areas, where the poor state of roads prevents women from using intermediate modes of transport (ex. rickshaws and bicycles) and forces them to travel on foot (Duchène, 2011[71]). This could be problematic for women because they tend to have programmes of activities that are more complex than those of men due to their double working day.

In developing countries, women have a perception of insecurity in public transport, which limits their mobility options and possibilities to access opportunities. It is not enough that opportunities are available for them if women do not perceive to be safe by using public transport they will simply not travel. For example, in Asunción and Lima, 75% and 80% of women respectively have a perception of insecurity while travelling in public transport, particularly at night (Jaitman, 2020[75]). This perception is higher among women who do not use public transport and belong to higher-income groups. In Asunción (24%) and Lima

(78%), women have witnessed or have been victims of crime while using public transport (Galiani and Jaitman, 2016[76]). In Mexico City, in 2018, a study showed that 88.5% of women who used public transport had been victims of at least one type of sexual harassment act and the perception of insecurity in public transport limits women's mobility options (SEMOVI, 2019[73]). To improve security for women and enhance accessibility, some cities reserve vehicles for women. In Brazil, Egypt, India, Japan, Mexico and the Philippines, some train coaches and areas on buses are for women only, in view of combating sexual harassment. In Dubai, India, Iran, Mexico and Russia, there are taxis reserved for women.

To enhance sustainable inclusive urbanisation, accessibility needs to be planned and fostered through a gender lens. For this purpose, there should be an understanding of the differences in how men and women interpret specific aspects of accessibility. For women, transport behaviour is more deeply shaped by socio-economic and life-stage factors than for men, thus the way women and men interpret accessibility in physical, cognitive, financial and emotional terms varies greatly and defines how they use transport (ITF, 2019[77]). Improving women's safety in public transport is essential to closing the gender gap in access to opportunities. Other aspects that would make a difference in enhancing accessibility from gender and inclusive perspective are: encouraging and funding the collection of disaggregated data to build a better evidence base for gender-sensitive planning; integrating gender into transport projects and funding with gender budgeting; and linking women's issues with transport, education and employment (Allen, 2019[70]; ITF, 2019[77])

The design, function and use of the transport system and urban environments should be planned considering the needs of all travellers equally to give everyone access to their city. It cannot be assumed that any transport investment and improvement will benefit everyone equally. Accessibility contributes to broader government objectives of well-being, sustainability and social inclusion by facilitating people's access to opportunities regardless of their age, abilities or disabilities, gender and socio-economic background. It has the potential to improve quality of life and helps lift people out of poverty. For that, cities need to improve their understanding of the links between accessibility, inclusiveness and well-being and of the travel patterns of women, the elderly, children, etc. This can only be achieved if the potential synergies between improving the access to goods, services and information, and goals such as environmental protection and limiting social exclusion are considered from the outset. Research has shown that women tend to use more bus services as it is easier to access opportunities at shorter distances than by train but if bus services are not designed and planned based on this logic and safety is not improved, this imposes a strong barrier in women's accessibility possibilities (Allen, 2019[70]).

Planning and designing smart mobility projects should go beyond technological considerations to ensure well-being, inclusiveness and accessibility. One way of doing so is by engaging the local community in the development of the smart mobility initiative or project as well as in its implementation. Local authorities are using smart city strategies to make cities safer, accessible and sustainable. For smart mobility projects to be inclusive, they also need to reduce the physical barriers to transport access for the elderly, disabled people, children, etc. Cities are implementing different projects to redesign stations and vehicles to facilitate physical access to transport for persons with reduced mobility regardless of gender and age. For example:

- Paris is ensuring the installation of sensors in metro stations to provide important sound information to sight-impaired users.[19]
- Madrid is using technological solutions via a contactless travel card for people with limited mobility to use public transport and parking areas.[20]
- London seeks to enhance streets and the public transport network to enable disabled and older people to travel more easily spontaneously and independently, making the transport system navigable and accessible to all and reducing the additional journey time that disabled and older users can experience.[21] TfL has already set ambitious aims to improve step-free access and is

working to make 40% of the tube network step-free by 2022 (a significant increase from the current 26%) (Greater London Authority, 2018[25]).

Promoting gender-inclusive urbanisation and transport requires the participation of a wider range of stakeholders, including women and disadvantaged groups (i.e. the elderly and minorities) in the transport sector. Women make up only 22% of the transport workforce in Europe (EC, 2017[78]). Taking affirmative action to promote gender equality in the transport sector may be a way to have more women involved in the transport sector. Mexico City's Strategic Plan of Gender and Mobility aims to reduce sexual harassment of women, strengthen gender parity in the transport sector and satisfy the specific mobility needs of women. It includes targets for the participation of women in the transport sector. By 2024, the plan aims to have at least 5% more women in positions at the Director-General level and in areas where women make up less than 30% of the workforce (SEMOVI, 2019[73]).

Cities need to harness the knowledge of citizens by providing win-win opportunities to gain their active participation in city transformation. The amount and variety of outreach carried out by cities and their transport authorities varies but there is a clear recognition across cities of the importance of community engagement. Cities and transport authorities view public engagement and customer service as core components of their transport and accessibility strategies. Citizens have different needs, preferences and opportunities to access various activities depending on several factors such as the stage in life, gender, income and perceptions on what is valuable.

Improving the quality of life through urban form

It is widely acknowledged that cities are not just centres of economic growth but need to consider concerns over quality of life such as equity, access to open space, services and goods, and environmental issues. However, it is becoming increasingly difficult to manage the interdependence of issues that cities must address. Although sectoral policies can help enhance quality of life, a focus on integrated policies is vital to tackle urban challenges. Focusing on urban form is a way of enhancing coherence across economic, social and environmental policies with an impact on quality of life and therefore accessibility.

Research suggests that well-designed urban form can be an effective tool to increase a sense of place and physical activity, improve air quality and accessibility, increase social cohesion and promote well-being among residents in urban areas (OECD, 2014[79]). The urban form is important because it contains four key interdependent metrics that contribute to high ridership and lower GHG emissions from public and private transport: density, land use mix, connectivity and a balanced transport offer (IPCC, 2014[14]). Cities' experience shows that investing in mass transit may help reduce congestion and GHG emissions, as well as contribute to well-being and competitiveness. However, public transit alone cannot increase ridership without significant geographic expansion and improved service levels (DeRobertis, 2010[80]). Ridership is more likely to increase when transport and the urban form are planned in parallel.

Urban density – Promoting sustainable development

Density refers to how intensively urban land is utilised and proximity particularly concerns the location of urban agglomerations in a metropolitan area (OECD, 2012[3]).[22] Cities with high levels of population density can more effectively serve their residents with rapid transit as fewer kilometres of infrastructure are needed to serve the same population (Marks, Mason and Oliveira, 2016[6]). High density (population, housing, jobs) levels are commonly associated with "compact city" strategies. Among several types of urban forms, the compact city has been presented as a way of encouraging urban sustainability as it promotes walkable, eco-friendly urban forms. Globally, cities are becoming denser; this densification accounts for 50% to 60% of the global city population growth (OECD/European Commission, 2020[2]). This increase in density requires more investments to provide housing, jobs and services such as transport.

The COVID-19 pandemic has reinforced the value of proximity by enhancing accessibility through urban design and planning (OECD, 2020[4]). With COVID-19, debates have started to emerge on the vulnerability of densely populated urban areas. They are regarded as places where the risk of contagion is higher than in low-density places. However, research has found that density is not significantly associated with COVID-19 infection rates, in fact, areas with high density tend to have lower death rates.[23] OECD research has concluded that "...it is not density alone that make cities vulnerable to COVID-19, but the structural economic and social conditions of cities make them more or less able to implement effective policy responses" (OECD, 2020, p. 15[4]).

Density levels vary depending on the income level of every country. Cities in low-income countries are 4 times denser than those in high-income countries; the population density in cities in North America is less than 2 000 inhabitants per km^2, whereas in South Asia and Sub-Saharan Africa, it is around 8 000 inhabitants per km^2 (OECD/European Commission, 2020[2]). Moreover, in Europe, cities with similar levels of population have very different densities, reflecting their differences in urbanisation patterns. For example, cities like Milan (73 people/hectare [ha]), Munich (44 people/ha), Prague (25 people/ha), Vienna (41 people/ha) and Warsaw (33 people/ha) with similar population levels differ in their levels of density (IPR, 2015[38]).

In most metropolitan areas, the majority of the residents live outside the city core and these people are in general not able to access opportunities by public transport nearly as well as residents in central areas (Marks, Mason and Oliveira (2016[6]). The problem is that urban growth tends to happen outside city centres where there is limited public transport service. Indeed, according to the European Commission and the OECD (2020[2]), the further away from the city centre, the lower the densities are, and the larger the city, the more distance is needed for densities to drop. In the Czech Republic, for instance, the build-up areas of cities have increased in recent years leading to urban sprawl and a process of suburbanisation as more people live in the suburbs than in the core areas. Suburbanisation is one of the causes of high levels of car ownership and in consequence heavy road traffic and air pollution as public transport options are limited in suburban areas (OECD, 2018[81]). Greater efforts are needed to allow for and encourage densification, in particular easing density restrictions in low-density areas close to city centres and along public transport corridors; this is key but gradual densification should also be permitted in most parts of an urban area (OECD, 2017[20]).

Many cities across the world are promoting policies towards more compact urban developments. In a compact city, urban land is intensively used, urban agglomerations are contiguous and there is a clear difference between rural and urban land (Table 1.2). Moreover, urban areas are linked by public transport systems that determine how effectively urban land is utilised (OECD, 2012[3]). Another characteristic of compact cities is that it facilitates access to local jobs and services. For that, land use is mixed and most residents have access to services and goods either by foot or by public transport. Research suggests that higher population densities, especially when combined with high employment densities, are strongly correlated with easier access to goods, services and information (IPCC, 2014[14]; OECD, 2012[3]). A lack of opportunities in the vicinity where people live cannot be overcome by greater transport efficiency. Conversely, in cities with low densities of employment, commerce and housing, there is generally an increase in the average travel distances for accessing opportunities. These longer travel distances also contribute to higher GHG emissions.

Table 1.2. Key characteristics of a compact city

Dense and proximate development patterns	Urban areas linked by public transport systems	Accessibility to local jobs and services
Urban land is intensively utilised Urban agglomerations are contiguous or close together Distinct border between urban and rural land use Public spaces are secured	Effective use of land Public transport systems facilitate mobility in urban areas	Land use is mixed Most residents have access to local services either on foot or by public transport

Source: Based on OECD (2012[3]), *Compact City Policies: A Comparative Assessment*, https://dx.doi.org/10.1787/9789264167865-en.

The effective management of density is key to promoting compact, well-planned cities. "Densification is perceived as a fundamental strategy for creating sustainable accessibility" (Gil Solá, Vilhelmson and Larsson, 2018[7]). The creation of high-density, mixed-use places requires transport investment to be fully aligned with the city's growth strategy. At a minimum, densification may be possible by easing land use restrictions such as restrictive zoning regulations and planning decisions that prevent it. Explicit restrictions such as floor-to-floor area rations or implicit restrictions such as minimum lot-size requirements and limitations on multifamily homes are just some practices that prevent densification (OECD, 2017[20]). Policies that promote compact cities tend to incentivise the development of brownfield over greenfield land. Higher density makes it easier for cities to promote mass transit, as it needs high density to pay off investments. Hence, density and mass transit must be planned jointly (DeRobertis, 2010[80]). Allowing high densities where there is no mass transit or allowing mass transit where there is low density is not likely to lead to better accessibility. The central goal is to promote high density in city centres where services and goods could be accessed by walking. The strategies may include the establishment of new residential areas or buildings. Some instruments to promote compact city development include: minimum density standards, mixed-use regulation and a density bonus for developers (Rode et al., 2014[5]).

Cities reach a level where increasing density is no longer desired. The aim is to reach a level of sufficient density and not maximising or increasing density as this could have negative effects, such as reducing well-being levels. In Paris, for example, increasing density levels could lead to higher demands on public services, insufficient water availability, poor air quality and waste disposal problems.

Cities tend to promote compact city development with a hierarchy of higher density and mixed-use clusters around public transport nodes. These strategies normally involve the redevelopment of areas in proximity to major transit stations. They intend to maximise access to transit through land use planning and community development policies. Examples can be found in cities such as London, Milan, Stuttgart and the Île-de-France region around Paris (Box 1.10). This is because the most significant influence on transit seems to be proximity to public transport. The neighbourhood around the stations is an essential part of the life of the city as the station is the link between public transport and the city. When a new public transport service (mostly rail transport) is provided in a neighbourhood, it has an impact on its functioning and planning. Cities such as London consider that land around stations provides opportunities to create high-density, mixed-use places that are well connected to local amenities, and jobs and locations further afield. This is a way to make the most of past public transport investment and the benefits of any future investment by providing new homes and jobs nearby. In the Île-de-France region, France, the development of the Grand Paris project places the *gare* (station) at the centre of urban development. Other examples include Denmark's Planning Act which requires new offices over 1 500 m^2 to be located within 600 metres of a rail station contributing to Copenhagen's compact urban form. Korean cities have also explored the integration of land use policy and transport policies to build more compact cities and make better use of available land, particularly as cities face critical urban challenges such as demographic change and access to affordable housing (Box 1.11).

Box 1.10. Accessibility in redeveloped urban areas – The cases of Île-de-France, London, Milan and Stuttgart

The old fairgrounds in **Milan**, Italy, occupied a large site (approximately 0.6 km^2) in a central location less than 3.5 km from the central station and the city centre. Due to its prime location, local authorities decided the site was better suited for mixed-use development. The project was called City Life. To build it, Milan amended its zoning plan to change the use from fairground to mixed-use, under the premise that the redeveloped area would be denser than the surrounding areas but with more parks and open spaces. This density/open space combination was achieved by concentrating residential uses in three 27-story towers. Roads were not extended through the project site, pedestrian and bicycle pathways were given priority making it the largest car-free area in Milan. All parking was built underground. Non-residential buildings, including museums, shops and offices were determined through public meetings and negotiations between local authorities and developers. Coincidentally, a new metro line had been sited near the project and city planners realigned the metro to include a new station underneath the project City Life. Moreover, city planners re-analysed the project's traffic and parking requirements and concluded that parking could be reduced to 1 000 from the 4 000 spaces originally planned.

The Möhringen station in **Stuttgart**, Germany, was historically a freight station and rail yard. As the city built its tramlines, the station became the core area linking the former village of Möhringen to the city centre. Eventually, the rail yard became obsolete and, in 1995, local authorities planned for its redevelopment. Stuttgart amended its 1990 general plan and selected densities consistent with other city areas with the same characteristics, even though Möhringen was much denser than the adjacent neighbourhood. In the zoning amendment, the city rezoned the abutting low-density housing to this same higher density. Planners considered locating it and the services required (supermarkets, kindergartens, senior residences, etc.) near a light rail station. The redeveloped area includes five buildings of four stories each for mixed use. Planners decided that all parking had to be underground, only public parking for visitors and shoppers is available in the street. Since the local authorities give priority to housing construction, there are no fees for residential projects.

In the UK's capital city **London**, the Mayor's Transport Strategy promotes exploring opportunities for development around the nearly 600 rail and tube stations to create high-density and mixed-use areas. Some of the measures include converting land use from low-density uses (retail parks, storage, parking, etc) to high-density, mixed-use development. It is expected that such change could act as a catalyst for the regeneration of town centres and neighbourhoods and play a role in revitalising high streets. Development around stations could provide opportunities for rental housing, as affordable housing is a key challenge for the city. Locating high-density housing within walking distance of stations means that residents will not only be well connected by rail or tube to employment opportunities but also to schools, hospitals and shops by public transport, walking or cycling. A key advantage is that land around stations is often owned by the transport authority (Transport for London, TfL), Network Rail and other public sector owners. This is seen as a good opportunity to increase housing delivery by making better use of underused land. The Transport Strategy suggests using buses and cycle links to encourage high-density development further from stations and, in that way, increase the catchment area of a station.

In France, the **Île-de-France** (IDF) region, in which Paris is located, has 437 stations, 399 of which are outside Paris (not including metro stations). Approximately 35% of inhabitants in the region live within a radius of 800 metres from a station and 83% within less than 2 000 metres. In the coming years, the IDF region plans to increase the service of public transport, using the attraction power of the stations to build new housing, bring new jobs and meet environmental objectives. The strategy is to increase density and the land use mix around stations. The urban mobility plans of the region call for better local planning of the urban public space around the stations and promote the use of public transport instead of the private car. One of the key actions is to build 68 new stations in areas that currently lack the service by 2030. These new stations are expected to increase the attractiveness of the neighbourhoods and contribute to their economic development. The Société du Grand Paris (SGP) (head of the transport project) launches a call for innovative projects on services or the planning of public spaces around stations every year. Regional and transport authorities promote a more coherent development around public transport infrastructure projects to achieve a more transversal development of the neighbourhoods around the stations. It is expected that this approach will be implemented in the extension of metro line 11 to the east of Paris and the extension of the RER E (suburban train) to the west (Mantes-la-Jolie). The different actors in charge of the suburban train extension have implemented an observatory of the territory to improve their knowledge of the urban development challenges and use it as a basis for discussions and decision-making. Similar projects around existing stations are in place.

Source: DeRobertis, M. (2010[80]), "Land development and transportation policies for transit-oriented development in Germany and Italy: Five case studies", http://www.gmfus.org/publications/land-development-and-transportation-policies-transit-oriented-development-germany-and (accessed on 9 July 2019); City Life Development (2017[82]), *City Life Project*, https://europe.uli.org/wp-content/uploads/sites/127/ULI-Documents/CityLife-Project.pdf; Successful policies on land use density, auto parking and assessment of transportation impacts, accessed at: Comparative Domestic Policy Fellowship German Marshall Fund (n.d.[83]), "Comparative Domestic Policy Fellowship", https://cittastadt.files.wordpress.com/2009/12/presentation-vta-dec09pdfreduced1.pdf; Greater London Authority (2018[25]), *Mayor's Transport Strategy*, http://www.london.gov.uk (accessed on 15 July 2019). For Île-de-France: Laurent, S. (2018[84]), *La gare au coeur du développement urbain*, https://www.iau-idf.fr/fileadmin/NewEtudes/Etude_1596/C175_web.pdf (accessed on 5 August 2019).

Urban redevelopment strategies are essential for the promotion of densification. It is commonly accepted that certain levels of density could contribute to economic growth due to increased agglomeration. Deteriorated buildings or areas could be repurposed for housing or other cultural or leisure activities boosting the economic activity of the area. But accessibility considerations should be part of the initiatives to make them effective. Public transport is a key component of policies intended to revitalise, regenerate and support growth in deprived areas (UITP, 2018[85]). People living in deprived areas most of the time rely on walking or public transport, when provided, for accessing jobs, goods and services. If public spaces and transport are undeveloped, they will have limited access to socio-economic opportunities. Co-ordinating investment in public transport and redevelopment projects has the potential of increasing access to opportunities and contribute to well-being.

Box 1.11. Enhancing sustainability through compact city policies – The experience of Korean cities

Korean cities face increasing challenges due to rapid urbanisation. The share of the urban population doubled from 40.7% in 1975 to 81.9% in 2009. Korea is one of the densest and most urbanised countries in the world. Korea's population is increasingly concentrated in urban areas. While the percentage of the global population residing in urban areas increased from 31% to 51% between 1960 and 2010, Korea's share of urban residents jumped from nearly 28% to 83% during the same period. The country's economic model and rapid growth underpinned by highly urbanised spatial form have led to increased resource consumption and put pressure on the environment. Today, Korean cities are characterised by smaller and ageing households. For instance, the ratio of single-person households increased from 5% in 1980 to 24% in 2010. Korea based its urban development largely on road-oriented transport (ROT), which increases energy consumption, air pollution and commuting distance.

For example, in Seoul Metropolitan Area (SMA), the average commuting distance increased from 9.7 km in 1996 to 13 km in 2010. Road construction doubled from 1990 to 2012, by which roadways accounted for approximately 10% of total urban area. In consequence, traffic congestion cost increased by 32% between 2003 and 2007 and accounted for 2.4% of the national GDP in 2010. Unequal public transport accessibility (in Seoul, 91.2% of people live within a 5-minute walk from public transport but only 68% in Daejeon), unequal job density (85.96% in Seoul, 58.95% in Incheon) and unbalanced matching index in local service accessibility (0.04 in Jung-gu/Seoul, 0.069 in Gangnam-gu/Seoul) show the need to change the urban form model. This requires the integration of public transport with urban form planning.

To face these challenges, Korean urban policy has evolved over time to promote urban compact city policies. The Korean government's Second Revision of the Fourth National Comprehensive Plan and other documents have acknowledged the need to make urban areas more compact by promoting high-density development and building affordable housing near railway stations. Mixed land use and integrating land use policy with transport policy through transport-oriented development strategies are alternatives that Korean cities are exploring to achieve sustainable urban development goals.

Source: OECD (2012[86]), *OECD Urban Policy Reviews, Korea 2012*, https://dx.doi.org/10.1787/9789264174153-en; OECD (2014[79]), *Compact City Policies: Korea: Towards Sustainable and Inclusive Growth*, https://dx.doi.org/10.1787/9789264225503-en.

Research suggests that excessive densification could reduce proximity and increase travel (Gil Solá, Vilhelmson and Larsson, 2018[7]). The problem is that building more housing may increase economic returns for land use but it may also crowd out less intensive land uses such as public meeting places, recreational areas, schools, etc. The need for new housing and related densification may threaten the quality of public spaces such as urban parks, green areas and playgrounds. Moreover, as has happened in some cities such as Prague and Vancouver, a side effect of densification is that it may exclude economically vulnerable groups. The reason is that a new high standard of housing may be relatively expensive to buy or rent for low-income households, which could be forced to move to peripheral areas with cheaper housing. In this case, these groups may not have the same access to goods and services as those living in central areas. The renovation of older housing near central areas well served by public transport may also create gentrification and exclude some low-income residents.

Research has found an overarching trend in the decline of population and built-up densities in cities across the world (IPCC, 2014[14]). According to OECD studies, "[d]espite growing populations and pressures on the housing market of many cities, little densification has occurred in recent decades in most urban areas in the OECD" (OECD, 2017, p. 23[20]). However, this decline varies across income groups, city sizes and regions.

A common misconception about density is that it requires high-rise buildings configured in close proximity to each other. This is the case in many Asian cities, particularly in the People's Republic of China (China hereafter), that rely on the vertical expansion of built-up areas. Multiple land use configurations can lead to the same levels of density. High population density does not necessarily mean high-rise buildings. One key point of consideration is that accessibility should focus on making everyday life easier for residents. Therefore, since most new buildings are inserted into already defined land uses, to make everyday life simpler would entail adding complementary activities that add value (Gil Solá, Vilhelmson and Larsson, 2018[7]). The challenge here is to focus on residents needs rather than only on the availability of land to build and promote activities that may not be in line with residents' priorities.

Integrating land use and transport policies

How land is used has a strong effect on the length of commutes, environmental sustainability and climate adaptation and mitigation efforts. Cities have an important role to play in land use planning, as this is mostly the purview of local governments across the OECD. Land use planning is place-based by definition and highly context-specific and thus requires a high level of information on local conditions, which higher levels of government often do not have (OECD, 2017[20]). Land use mix refers to the diversity and integration of land uses (i.e. parks, residential, commercial, industrial). The land use mix can be measured in several ways: i) the ratio of jobs to residents; ii) the variety and mixture of amenities and activities; and iii) the proportion of retail and housing (IPCC, 2014[14]). Therefore, diverse and mixed land uses can reduce travel distances and enable walking and other active modes of transport to access goods and services (Kockelman, 1997[87]; OECD, 2017[20]). However, some research suggests that the politics of land use and transportation decisions rarely favours accessibility as an important policy outcome (Duranton and Guerra, 2016[16]).

Land use policy and transport policy are normally integrated through transit-oriented development (TOD) strategies. TOD planning should cover diverse scales, not only small land plots around stations. TOD planning on a large scale is a way to ensure a sufficient number of public transit customers and to justify the investment in public transport (OECD, 2014[79]; DeRobertis, 2010[80]). For example, in 2004, the Hammarby Sjöstad neighbourhood in southern Stockholm set itself the goal of increasing public transport ridership, bicycle use or walking by 80% by 2010. By 2008, ridership had already increased to 79% due to increases in the number of residents (OECD, 2014[79]). Its tram line was built as the main commuting traffic mode and the first tram line ever to serve as a connection between the southern neighbourhoods of Stockholm. Other features of the local transport system include its pedestrian and bicycle network, its large carpooling system and the ferry system (Perth and Berg, 2014[88]).[24] In Metro Vancouver, municipalities and regional authorities use the concept of Frequent Transit Network (FTN) to identify corridors linking urban centres and other key activity areas with high-frequency, high-quality service. Whether served by bus, rail or ferry, FTN corridors – and especially the nodes where these corridors intersect – are important places for the region to direct growth and development. The FTN has become an important organising framework in Metro Vancouver for co-ordinating land use and transport policies.

One key lesson from the experience of Metro Vancouver is that, to improve accessibility, it is necessary to rethink transport. To deliver the Regional Transport Strategy of the metro area, the transport authority, TransLink, needs to invest strategically to maintain and expand the transport system. For that, investment decisions are made in tandem with decisions on land use and demand management. The key issue is to ensure that new projects enhance goods movement and travel time reliability without increasing general purpose traffic; therefore, understanding what land uses are in place and current and future demand is essential. Where basic networks are incomplete or supply is insufficient to meet demand, decisions on the expansion are made in a way that promotes regional goals as cost-effectively as possible. TransLink has noticed that infrastructure alone cannot resolve transportation problems, especially if new infrastructure acts to encourage people to travel farther or more frequently.

The provision of strategic infrastructure is a critical element that determines the character of a city at any stage of development. Public transport and services determine urban mobility patterns including modal choice. That is why infrastructure developments should be directly linked to strategic planning policy, which in turn informs local planning and regulation (Rode et al., 2014[5]). This is, however, not always easy, as linking transport to land use and strategic planning depends on the level of maturity and capacity of the institutional planning framework of the region or city. That is probably one of the reasons why cities in less developed countries focus exclusively on trying to satisfy transport demand and the provision of infrastructure without necessary considering other urban development issues.

One of the best-known examples of urban containment land use regulations and TOD is the Finger Plan of Copenhagen's Capital Region (Box 1.12). The Finger Plan is a national planning directive that sets the overall principles for municipal planning in the Greater Copenhagen area. It requires that municipal planning be carried out based on an assessment of development in the area as a whole and must ensure that the main principles of the overall "finger city" structure are continued. The main lesson from this plan is the importance of co-ordinating urban development with the expansion of infrastructure such as transport. Thus, under this plan, the principle of accessibility is a key element of controlling sprawl and maintaining a compact urban form. For instance, the plan provides that large office workplaces should generally be located within 600 metres of the closest public transport stations (Danish Ministry of the Environment, 2015[89]).

Box 1.12. Ensuring an overall regional planning strategy: Copenhagen's Finger Plan

In 1947, the Danish Regional Planning Office created Copenhagen's Finger Plan. Since its adoption, the plan has been the backbone of regional planning for the Greater Copenhagen area even though different bodies have carried out the planning and with different legal effects. Through the Finger Plan, planners have sought to establish urban growth on the basis of an overall structure where urban development is concentrated along city fingers linked to the railway system and radial road networks, and the city fingers are separated by green "wedges" which are protected from urban development. Currently, the area covered by overall planning for the Greater Copenhagen area includes 34 municipalities.

The Finger Plan is a national planning directive issued pursuant to the Planning Act. According to the plan, urban development of regional significance must be co-ordinated with the expansion of overall infrastructure within the Greater Copenhagen area with special consideration for public transport services. The municipal planning in the Greater Copenhagen area must ensure that:

- Urban development and urban regeneration in the core urban region take place within the existing urban zone and with consideration for the opportunities to strengthen public transport services.
- Urban development and new urban functions in the peripheral urban region (the "finger city") must be located with consideration for existing and approved infrastructure and the opportunities to strengthen public transport.
- The green "wedges" are not converted into urban zones or used as recreational facilities.
- Urban development in the rest of the Greater Copenhagen area is local in nature and takes place in connection with municipal centres.

The plan also ensures that overall areas significant for the development of the metropolitan area as a whole are reserved for future transport infrastructure, technical installations, noise impact areas, etc.

Source: Danish Ministry of the Environment (2015[89]), *The Finger Plan - A Strategy for the Development of the Greater Copenhagen Area*, http://www.naturstyrelsen.dk (accessed on 19 July 2019).

For cities with less mixed land use, such as those in Asia and North America, large residential developments are separated from jobs and retail centres by long distances. In cities with more space dedicated to single-use areas, residents tend to travel overall longer distances and carry out a larger share of their travel in private vehicles than residents who live in areas with more land in mixed use. Low levels of mixed land use increase commuting distances and have a negative impact on social cohesion and city productivity levels. This is the case of several cities in Latin America, where the pattern of land use has led to the hollowing out of city centres and moved population to the suburbs away from jobs and services. In

Mexico, for instance, urbanisation does not translate into economic development because cities fail to provide an environment that connects inhabitants to economic opportunities and to social and urban infrastructure, and prevents firms from reaping agglomeration benefits (Box 1.13). In this case, as in many other developing cities, institutions governing land use may only mature enough over time to effectively regulate land markets and manage land conversions.

Box 1.13. Poor land use planning limits access to jobs and services: The case of Mexican cities

Urban expansion in Mexican metropolitan areas has been inefficient and costly, hollowing out city centres and contributing to social segregation. In the last decades, urban development occurred at ever greater distances from the centre city and became increasingly spatially dispersed rather than clustered. Moreover, roughly 90% of the housing stock consists of individual homes rather than denser and multi-family residences, and individual homes continue to make up the majority of all new development. Other factors have played a role: rising income levels and lower transport costs; a fiscal and regulatory bias towards single-family, owner-occupied homes; the prevalence of irregular settlements; weak municipal capacity and local land use controls for urban development; and a high level of municipal fragmentation within metropolitan areas, making co-ordinated land use and transport planning across neighbouring jurisdictions a challenge.

Urban sprawl has had significant consequences for mobility. It has contributed to rising rates of car ownership and making the provision of efficient, quality public transport alternatives more challenging and costly. Mexico's motorisation rate doubled over the past decade, reaching 20 vehicles per 100 people and, in 2011, over 70% of the country's 22.4 million cars were registered in metropolitan zones. Public transport service, consisting primarily of buses, can be unreliable, expensive and time-consuming, and the fleet is often of poor quality. The development of bus rapid transit (BRT) networks in some cities is promising, yet too often remains divorced from broader urban planning efforts.

Source: OECD (2015[90]), *OECD Urban Policy Reviews: Mexico 2015: Transforming Urban Policy and Housing Finance*, https://dx.doi.org/10.1787/9789264227293-en.

The experience of Germany and the US suggests that linking national urban transport funds to integrated urban planning has proven useful to increase co-ordination of urban transport and land use planning (Aguilar Jaber and Glocker, 2015[91]). In the US New Starts programme, project sponsor agencies are required by the Federal Transit Administration (FTA) to submit information of existing land use, transit-supportive plans and policies, performance and impacts of policies. In Germany, planning procedures involving interest groups and the public are part of the requirements to access national funds for urban transport projects. Developing an environmental impact assessment and a cost-benefit analysis are part of these requirements (Aguilar Jaber and Glocker, 2015[91]). Linking national urban transport funds to integrated urban planning can also pay off in emerging economies. In India, for example, this has been facilitated by national funds made available for urban transport projects as part of a larger urban development project and funded by the Ministry of Urban Development. In order to be eligible for funding, transport projects have to be part of a comprehensive city development plan (Aguilar Jaber and Glocker, 2015[91]).

The effectiveness of land use policy towards higher densities and mixed use depends on the willingness of residents to accept high levels of density by changing from using private cars to public transport and non-motorised modes of transportation (Inturri et al., 2017[12]). Certainly, the level of service is also a determinant on changing people's behaviour towards using transport. Traffic congestion, little diffusion of cycling and walking for systematic trips, the inefficiency of parking management and the absence of city logistics measures are some of the factors that may affect people's transport behaviour and perception. Another problem is that, in general, when land uses are planned without co-ordination across policy sectors, the distance between origin and destination tend to be longer (IPCC, 2014[14]).

Connectivity – Building pedestrian-friendly cities

Many modern cities have to contend with two legacies from earlier planning: the distribution of single-use land zones and the promotion of car dependency. Planners today wish to correct those errors by increasing densities, promoting mixed land use and increasing connectivity. Connectivity refers to street density and design and can be measured by block size, or intersections per road kilometre (IPCC, 2014[14]). A high level of street connectivity is characterised by finer grain systems with smaller blocks that allow frequent changes in direction. It has a positive correlation with the convenience of walking and lower GHG emissions. Low street connectivity has certainly the opposite effect. The human-scale street design includes smaller block sizes, higher building densities and mixed-use to facilitate micro-accessibility, last-mile connectivity, walkability and social interaction (Rode et al., 2014[5]). In China, for instance, cities have low levels of density and Chinese planners are well aware of (and often advocate) multifunctional zoning but a clear separation of functions prevails. The OECD (2015[92]) concluded that if China is to build denser, more liveable cities it should work more on connectivity.

Box 1.14. Building more liveable urban areas: The case of Chinese cities

Improving the quality of urbanisation in Chinese cities requires promoting more pedestrian-friendly cities. Chinese cities are characterised by the existence of superblocks that discourage walking and community life. Chinese authorities need to do more than simply pursuing increased densities, which might in any case overload infrastructure systems and have other undesired consequences. Some of the actions that Chinese cities could do to improve the quality of city life are:

- Chinese cities need to improve internal connectivity by developing finer-grained road networks. The number of road intersections per square kilometre in Chinese cities is drastically lower than in Western cities and the distance between intersections is anywhere from three to ten times greater. Breaking up the superblocks would create more competition among small developers and also facilitate the formation of denser, more vibrant urban communities. This requires more flexible zoning to allow for more mixed-use development. The problem is that, currently, the massive grid of roads 50 to 60 metres wide (more similar to motorways than city streets) segments the urban space, while large square blocks with just 1 or 2 entrances further reduces internal connectivity.
- Density could be managed at smaller scales than the superblock, allowing gradual densification to be co-ordinated with infrastructure development, for instance by allowing higher densities closer to metro stations and other public transport interchanges, in line with the principles of TOD.

Source: OECD (2015[92]), *OECD Urban Policy Reviews: China 2015*, https://dx.doi.org/10.1787/9789264230040-en.

Improving on low levels of connectivity in cities is complex and expensive. As infrastructure already exists, increasing connectivity requires investment either to redevelop the site or a retrofit to facilitate walking and cycling. Street patterns may need to be redesigned for smaller blocks with high connectivity. Retrofitting often involves widening sidewalks, constructing medians and adding bike lanes, as well as reducing traffic speeds, improving traffic signals and providing parking for bicycles (IPCC, 2014[14]). Improving connectivity levels also has a political cost, which could be bigger than the economic one. Decision-makers need to balance the preferences of those who lobby for a more pedestrian-friendly city with active mobility options and those who depend on the private car to commute and have a need for parking spaces. This is a difficult balance to achieve; thus decision-makers would need to be willing to pay the political cost of any decision in either direction.

Actions to correct past planning errors must be based on the unique historic, cultural, geographic and climate variables of every city and account for how people choose to live. In Australia and Mexico for instance, people generally prefer living in single housing units. Thus, retrofitting existing cities with high-density activity centres, and corridors and transit-oriented developments may not be workable ideas in all contexts. For instance, in Perth, Australia, isolated apartment enclaves, apartments lining highways, crammed unit developments and high-rise developments in low-rise town centres are emerging across the city and less than 10% of people living within walking distance of a train station actually use it for travelling (Lutton, 2017[93]). The lesson from the Australian experience in city retrofitting is that higher densities and public transport of themselves do not improve quality of life but their planning must respect the unique and physical context of a city through meaningful local community participation (Lutton, 2017[93]). In Mexico, people largely prefer living in a single-family home rather than in flats but the convenience of proximity to services in central areas is leading to a change in preference among younger generations who would prefer living in a flat in central areas.

Changing the balance between modes of transport

Accessibility requires offering different mobility alternatives (transport solutions). Accessibility planning requires a balance between various transport modes by promoting public transit, walking and cycling, while car use should be deemphasised or even reduced in some areas. Most city planners appear to be in favour of promoting public transit, cycling and walking, mainly by changing land use and urban structures. However, this does not mean that the use of cars is to be abolished or reduced by planning. The question is more about changing the balance between different modes of transport, a change that might even lead to better conditions for certain car users, such as less congestion. Changes in land use and the transportation system could result in changes in the accessibility conditions (Straatemeier, 2008[8]).

Research suggests that given the strong interrelationship between urban form and transport, the integration of land use and transport represents a unique opportunity to enhance accessibility and more sustainable planning outcomes (Rode et al., 2014[5]). The concept of accessibility provides a basis for making trade-offs between land use and transport policies that has been sorely lacking. Accessibility gives planners the opportunity to assess the impact changes in transport and land use system has on the potential for interaction offered by different places in the urban network (Straatemeier, 2008[8]). Research suggests that in cities where motorisation is already mature, changing accessibility no longer influences car-dependent lifestyles and travel behaviours. This means that regions at the early stages of urbanisation have a unique opportunity to influence accessibility, in particular in cases where income levels, infrastructure and motorisation trends are changing rapidly (IPCC, 2014[14]).

Enhancing accessibility requires a planning approach with a broader perspective on planning than just transport. This means it should include other instruments of planning and areas of urban development. For planners in the Metro Vancouver Regional District, the best transport plan is a good land use plan; but based on the case studies elaborated for this report and the evidence gathered through research, it is possible to argue that a good accessibility policy is a good regional/metropolitan integrated development strategy. The reason is that accessibility is an objective that can only be achieved by the inclusion of different policy instruments: mobility (transport), land use, housing, etc. For that, cities need to identify how best to sequence, co-ordinate and integrate various transport infrastructure investments with land use development. This planning approach also provides an opportunity to improve social inclusion by prioritising housing and infrastructure provision for lower-income households (Rode et al., 2014[5]).

Box 1.15. The case of accessibility in the Netherlands

In the Netherlands, following the hypothesis that increased access to opportunities favours new economic development, one could wonder if the expansion of road and rail capacity between Almere and Amsterdam is the best solution. Notwithstanding the positive effects of cutting down congestion levels, expanding existing infrastructure will not significantly increase the potential accessibility of Almere. Investing in new infrastructure connecting Almere to other neighbouring regions, to which it is currently not well connected, could have a much greater effect on the total number of available opportunities.

It is important to understand that accessibility works both ways, as Amsterdam would also benefit from improving accessibility between the two cities. A better solution could be to increase the network position of Almere by building new infrastructure connection to other parts of the region rather than just to Amsterdam and thus improving both its absolute and relative accessibility.

The interventions would not aim at increasing network efficiency but are aimed at increasing the number of opportunities available within a certain time budget. This results in two types of strategies. First, interventions in the transport system aimed at creating the right accessibility conditions in locations where particular spatial development is favoured. Second, signalling opportunities for spatial development at places in the urban network that already provide favourable accessibility conditions. This implies that planning for accessibility does not only refer to planning for shorter travel distances, as is often interpreted within transportation planning, but also to planning for social and economic interaction.

Source: Straatemeier, T. (2008[8]), "How to plan for regional accessibility?", http://dx.doi.org/10.1016/j.tranpol.2007.10.002.

There are examples of how transport can be linked to other urban development objectives. For example, in Paris, the *Grand Paris* project includes a transport component that places emphasis on improving the quality of mobility in the metropolitan area. It seeks to provide users with a wide range of transport solutions so that they can personalise their routes based on their location and information they receive. Although this mobility plan focuses on the infrastructure and the quality of the transport service, other plans and projects complement it by focusing on the revitalisation of the areas around the stations. In Metro Vancouver, the metropolitan transport authority, TransLink and the Regional Planning Authority have worked in co-ordination to develop the Regional Growth Strategy which underpins the regional transport plan (Box 1.16). This has allowed local authorities to develop the concept of "complete communities", understood as walkable, mixed-use, transit-oriented communities.

Box 1.16. Developing complete communities – Vancouver

In the Metro Vancouver Regional District, the development of "complete communities" is one of the strategic goals of both the Regional Growth Strategy (RGS) and Regional Transportation Strategy (RTS). Complete communities are understood as walkable, mixed-use, transit-oriented communities where people can work, access services, live and enjoy social, cultural, educational and recreational pursuits. Providing diverse and affordable housing choices to meet current and future demand is central to the idea of complete communities. Access to a wide range of services and amenities close to home and a strong sense of regional and community identity and connection are also considered important to promote health and well-being. An important strategy in the setting of complete communities is to design neighbourhoods within urban areas, urban centres and local centres that are accessible for people of all ages and physical ability, promote transit, cycling and walking. However, the implementation of the initiative is perhaps its weakest point as local councils need to do this individually, but still require support provided by Metro Vancouver.

In Metro Vancouver, residents have an increasing amount of choice in how to get around. More than 90% of the places where people live and work can be reached by public transport at higher levels than cities of comparable size in North America. Based on its compact model, it is estimated that the most affordable and efficient way of achieving liveability, environmental and economic goals is to ensure that, by 2045, half of all trips in the region are made by walking, cycling and transit as they are the lowest-cost and lowest-impact forms of transport. In Metro Vancouver, sustainable urban development is being shaped around the transit-oriented development (TOD) approach. TOD is considered an effective way of concentrating growth on brownfield sites while generating and attracting transit ridership to shift mode share.

Source: TransLink (2013[94]). (2013), *Regional Transportation Strategy: Strategic Framework, TransLink, Vancouver,* https://www.translink.ca/-/media/Documents/plans_and_projects/regional_transportation_strategy/ (accessed on 29 March 2018).

References

Aguilar Jaber, A. and D. Glocker (2015), "Shifting towards Low Carbon Mobility Systems", *International Transport Forum Discussion Papers*, No. 2015/17, OECD Publishing, Paris, https://doi.org/10.1787/5jrvzrjggnhh-en (accessed on 27 August 2019). [91]

Allen, H. (2019), "Women's mobility is defined by transport connectivity and accessibility", in *Transport Connectivity: A Gender Perspective*, OECD Publishing, Paris, https://www.itf-oecd.org/sites/default/files/docs/transport-connectivity-gender-perspective.pdf. [70]

Anable, J. and P. Goodwin (2018), "Assessing the Net Overall Distributive Effect of a Congestion Charge", *International Transport Forum Discussion Papers*, No. 2018/13, OECD Publishing, Paris, https://doi.org/10.1787/7f4c51f2-en. [59]

BEA (2020), *GDP & Personal Income [Database]*, https://apps.bea.gov/iTable/index_nipa.cfm. [26]

BMU (2018), *Incentives for Electric Vehicles in Norway*, Federal Ministry for the Environment, Nature Conservation and Nuclear Safety. [62]

Carbon Pricing Leadership Coalition (2016), *What Are the Options for Using Carbon Pricing Revenues?*. [96]

City Life Development (2017), *City Life Project*, https://europe.uli.org/wp-content/uploads/sites/127/ULI-Documents/CityLife-Project.pdf. [82]

City of Copenhagen (2011), *The City of Copenhagen's Bicycle Strategy 2011-2025*, http://www.kk.dk/cityofcyclists (accessed on 27 July 2020). [45]

City of Gothenburg (2014), *Gothenburg 2035 - Transport Strategy for a Close-Knit City*, Urban Transport Committee, City of Gothenburg, https://goteborg.se/wps/wcm/connect/6c603463-f0b8-4fc9-9cd4-c1e934b41969/Trafikstrategi_eng_140821_web.pdf?MOD=AJPERES (accessed on 16 July 2019). [72]

City of Malmö (2016), *Sustainable Urban Mobility Plan: Creating a More Sustainable Malmö*, City Council of Malmö, https://malmo.se/download/18.16ac037b154961d0287384d/1491301288704/Sustainable+urban+mobility+plan%28TROMP%29_ENG.pdf (accessed on 16 July 2019). [24]

CiViTAS (2013), *Enabling Cycling Cities: Ingredients for Success*, CiViTAS MIMOSA, http://www.pas-port.info/cycling (accessed on 3 June 2020). [55]

Coppola, P. and E. Papa (2013), "Accessibility planning tools for sustainable and integrated land use/transport (LUT) development: An application to Rome", *Procedia - Social and Behavioral Sciences*, Vol. 87, pp. 133-146, http://dx.doi.org/10.1016/j.sbspro.2013.10.599. [9]

CRTM (2016), *Annual Report 2016*, Consorcio Regional de Transportes de Madrid, Madrid, http://www.crtm.es (accessed on 19 October 2018). [32]

CRTM (2013), *Madrid, A World Reference - The Public Transport System in the Region of Madrid*, Consorcio Regional de Transportes de Madrid, Madrid, https://www.crtm.es/media/157716/wreference-2013nov-web.pdf (accessed on 22 October 2018). [40]

CRTM (2013), *Plan Estratégico de Movilidad Sostenible de la Comunidad de Madrid 2013-2025*, Consorcio Regional de Transportes de Madrid, Madrid, http://www.crtm.es/plan-estrategico-movilidad-sostenible (accessed on 2 October 2018). [41]

Curtis, C. (2008), "Planning for sustainable accessibility: The implementation challenge", *Transport Policy*, Vol. 15/2, pp. 104-112, http://dx.doi.org/10.1016/J.TRANPOL.2007.10.003. [11]

Danish Ministry of the Environment (2015), *The Finger Plan - A Strategy for the Development of the Greater Copenhagen Area*, http://www.naturstyrelsen.dk (accessed on 19 July 2019). [89]

DeRobertis, M. (2010), "Land development and transportation policies for transit-oriented development in Germany and Italy: Five case studies", German Marshall Fund of the United States, http://www.gmfus.org/publications/land-development-and-transportation-policies-transit-oriented-development-germany-and (accessed on 9 July 2019). [80]

Dewita, Y., M. Burke and B. Yen (2019), "The relationship between transport, housing and urban form: Affordability of transport and housing in Indonesia", *Case Studies on Transport Policy*, pp. 1-11, http://dx.doi.org/10.1016/j.cstp.2019.01.004. [23]

Diamond, R. (2016), "The determinants and welfare implications of US Workers' diverging location choices by skill: 1980-2000", *American Economic Review*, American Economic Association, http://dx.doi.org/10.1257/aer.20131706. [97]

Duchène, C. (2011), *Gender and Transport*, OECD Publishing, Paris, https://doi.org/10.1787/5kg9mq47w59w-en (accessed on 4 March 2020). [71]

Duranton, G. and E. Guerra (2016), "Urban accessibility: Balancing land use and transportation", University of Pennsylvania, https://faculty.wharton.upenn.edu/wp-content/uploads/2017/05/Urban-accessibility-Balancing-land-use-and-transportation-Gilles.pdf (accessed on 3 April 2018). [16]

EC (2017), *2017 Report on Equality between Women and Men in the EU*, European Commission, http://dx.doi.org/10.2838/258611. [78]

EC/UN-Habitat (2016), *The State of European Cities 2016 - Cities Leading the Way to a Better Future*, European Commission, http://dx.doi.org/10.2776/770065. [37]

Florczak, M. (2012), "Integration without regulations", https://fsr.eui.eu/wp-content/uploads/121207_Florczak_Maciej.pdf (accessed on 9 August 2019). [42]

Galiani, S. and L. Jaitman (2016), "El transporte público desde una perspectiva de género: Percepción de inseguridad y victimización en Asunción y Lima", BIB, https://publications.iadb.org/publications/spanish/document/El-transporte-p%C3%BAblico-desde-una-perspectiva-de-g%C3%A9nero-Percepci%C3%B3n-de-inseguridad-y-victimizaci%C3%B3n-en-Asunci%C3%B3n-y-Lima.pdf (accessed on 4 March 2020). [76]

German Marshall Fund (n.d.), "Comparative Domestic Policy Fellowship", https://cittastadt.files.wordpress.com/2009/12/presentation-vta-dec09pdfreduced1.pdf. [83]

Gil Solá, A., B. Vilhelmson and A. Larsson (2018), "Understanding sustainable accessibility in urban planning: Themes of consensus, themes of tension", *Journal of Transport Geography*, Vol. 70, pp. 1-10, http://dx.doi.org/10.1016/j.jtrangeo.2018.05.010. [7]

Greater London Authority (2018), *Mayor's Transport Strategy*, http://www.london.gov.uk (accessed on 15 July 2019). [25]

Hawkins Kreps, B. (2018), "A modest investment with major dividends: Cycling culture in the Netherlands", Resilience, https://www.resilience.org/stories/2018-11-08/a-modest-investment-with-major-dividends-cycling-culture-in-the-netherlands/ (accessed on 27 July 2020). [48]

IAU (2016), "L'évolution des modes de vie accroît le temps passé à se déplacer", *Note Rapide d'Institut d'Aménagement et d'Urbanisme*, Vol. 714. [67]

IEA (2019), *CO2 Emissions from Fuel Combustion 2019 - Highlights*, IEA, Paris, https://doi.org/10.1787/2a701673-en. [56]

Inturri, G. et al. (2017), "Influence of accessibility, land use and transport policies on the transport energy dependence of a city", *Transportation Research Procedia*, Vol. 25, pp. 3273-3285, http://dx.doi.org/10.1016/J.TRPRO.2017.05.165. [12]

IPCC (2014), *2014: Human settlements, infrastructure and spatial planning*, Cambridge University Press, Cambridge, United Kingdom and New York, NY, USA, https://www.ipcc.ch/site/assets/uploads/2018/02/ipcc_wg3_ar5_chapter12.pdf (accessed on 17 July 2019). [14]

IPR (2015), *Do You Know Prague? The City in Maps, Graphs and Figures*, IPR, http://www.iprpraha.cz/uploads/assets/dokumenty/obecne/do_you_know_prague.pdf. [38]

ITF (2020), *COVID-19 Transport Brief: Re-spacing Our Cities For Resilience*, International Transport Forum, https://www.itf-oecd.org/sites/default/files/respacing-cities-resilience-covid-19.pdf (accessed on 25 November 2020). [49]

ITF (2020), *Safe Micromobility*, ITF, Paris, https://www.itf-oecd.org/sites/default/files/docs/safe-micromobility_1.pdf (accessed on 21 September 2020). [47]

ITF (2019), "Benchmarking Accessibility in Cities: Measuring the Impact of Proximity and Transport Performance", *International Transport Forum Policy Papers*, No. 68, OECD Publishing, Paris, https://doi.org/10.1787/4b1f722b-en. [18]

ITF (2019), "Improving Transport Planning and Investment through the use of Accessibility Indicators", *International Transport Forum Policy Papers*, No. 66, OECD Publishing, Paris, https://doi.org/10.1787/46ddbcae-en (accessed on 16 July 2019). [10]

ITF (2019), *ITF Transport Outlook 2019*, OECD Publishing, Paris, https://dx.doi.org/10.1787/transp_outlook-en-2019-en. [60]

ITF (2019), *Transport Connectivity A Gender Perspective*, OECD Publishing, Paris, https://www.itf-oecd.org/sites/default/files/docs/transport-connectivity-gender-perspective.pdf (accessed on 28 July 2020). [77]

ITF (2018), *Integrating Urban Public Transport Systems and Cycling*, ITF Roundtable Reports, OECD Publishing, Paris, https://doi.org/10.1787/bd177112-en (accessed on 21 September 2020). [46]

ITF (2018), *Policy Priorities for Decarbonising Urban Passenger Transport*, ITF, Paris. [61]

ITF (2017), *ITF Transport Outlook 2017*, OECD Publishing, Paris, https://doi.org/10.1787/9789282108000-en. [58]

ITF (2017), "Linking People and Places: New ways of understanding spatial access in cities", *International Transport Forum Policy Papers*, No. 35, OECD Publishing, Paris, https://doi.org/10.1787/996cc49e-en. [19]

ITF/OECD (2020), "Leveraging digital technology and data for human-centric smart cities: The case of smart mobility", OECD, Paris. [66]

Jaitman, L. (2020), "Public transport from a gender perspective: Insecurity and victimization in Latin America. The case of Lima and Asuncion metropolitan areas", *Journal of Economics, Race, and Policy*, Vol. 3/1, pp. 24-40, http://dx.doi.org/10.1007/s41996-019-00040-2. [75]

Kahn, M. (2007), "Gentrification trends in new transit-oriented communities: Evidence from 14 cities that expanded and built rail transit systems", *Real Estate Economics*, Vol. 35/2, pp. 155-182, http://dx.doi.org/10.1111/j.1540-6229.2007.00186.x. [34]

Kockelman, K. (1997), "Travel behavior as function of accessibility, land use mixing, and land use Balance: Evidence from San Francisco Bay Area", *Transportation Research Record: Journal of the Transportation Research Board*, Vol. 1607/1, pp. 116-125, http://dx.doi.org/10.3141/1607-16. [87]

Laurent, S. (2018), *La gare au coeur du développement urbain*, pp. 30-33, https://www.iau-idf.fr/fileadmin/NewEtudes/Etude_1596/C175_web.pdf (accessed on 5 August 2019). [84]

Link (n.d.), *Intermodal Passenger Transport in Europe: Passenger Intermodality from A to Z*, European Forum on Intermodal Passenger Travel, http://www.rupprecht-consult.eu/uploads/tx_rupprecht/LINK_Guidance_Brochure.pdf. [31]

Lutton, L. (2017), "Retrofitted cities are forcing residents to live with planning failures – We're due for a rethink", The Conversation, http://theconversation.com/retrofitted-cities-are-forcing-residents-to-live-with-planning-failures-were-due-for-a-rethink-83216 (accessed on 10 September 2019). [93]

Manning, A. and B. Petrongolo (2017), "How local are labor markets? Evidence from a spatial job search model", *American Economic Review*, Vol. 107/10, pp. 2877-2907. [29]

Marks, M., J. Mason and G. Oliveira (2016), *People Near Transit: Improving Accessibility and Rapid Transit Coverage in Large Cities*, ITDP, https://3gozaa3xxbpb499ejp30lxc8-wpengine.netdna-ssl.com/wp-content/uploads/2016/10/People-Near-Transit.pdf (accessed on 12 March 2018). [6]

McKinsey & Company (2014), *Electric Vehicles in Europe: Gearing Up for a New Phase?*. [63]

Metro Vancouver (2017), *Transit-oriented Affordable Housing Study 2017-2019*, http://www.metrovancouver.org/services/regional-planning/housing-affordability/transit-oriented/Pages/default.aspx (accessed on 25 June 2018). [27]

Metro Vancouver (2015), *The Metro Vancouver Housing and Transportation Cost Burden Study - A New Way of Looking at Affordability*, Metro Vancouver, Vancouver, http://www.metrovancouver.org/services/regional-planning/PlanningPublications/HousingAndTransportCostBurdenReport2015.pdf (accessed on 29 June 2018). [22]

Mexico City Government (2014), *Ley de Movilidad del Distrito Federal*, Asamblea Legislativa del Distrito Federal, http://www.paot.org.mx/centro/leyes/df/pdf/2018/LEY_MOVILIDAD_DISTRITO_FEDERAL_02_04_2018.pdf (accessed on 9 September 2019). [15]

Moretti, E. (2012), *The New Geography of Jobs*, Houghton Mifflin Harcourt. [98]

Morton, C., R. Lovelace and J. Anable (2017), "Exploring the effect of local transport policies on the adoption of low emission vehicles: Evidence from the London congestion charge and hybrid electric vehicles", *Transport Policy*, Vol. 60, pp. 34-46. [64]

NSW Government (2018), *Future Transport Strategy 2056*, Transport for NSW, Sydney, https://future.transport.nsw.gov.au/sites/default/files/media/documents/2018/Future_Transport_2056_Strategy.pdf. [53]

NYC Department of Transportation (2016), *New York City Strategic Plan 2016*, Department of Transportation, New York, https://www.nycdotplan.nyc/PDF/Strategic-plan-2016.pdf (accessed on 6 August 2019). [17]

OECD (2020), "City policy responses", *Tackling Coronavirus (COVID-19): Contributing to a Global Effort*, OECD, Paris, https://read.oecd-ilibrary.org/view/?ref=126_126769-yen45847kf&title=Coronavirus-COVID-19-Cities-Policy-Responses. [4]

OECD (2019), *Accelerating Climate Action: Refocusing Policies Through a Well-Being Lens - Highlights*, OECD, Paris. [57]

OECD (2019), *OECD Regional Outlook 2019: Leveraging Megatrends for Cities and Rural Areas*, OECD Publishing, Paris, https://doi.org/10.1787/9789264312838-en. [65]

OECD (2018), *OECD Environmental Performance Reviews: Czech Republic 2018*, OECD Environmental Performance Reviews, OECD Publishing, Paris, https://dx.doi.org/10.1787/9789264300958-en. [81]

OECD (2017), *Gaps and Governance Standards of Public Infrastructure in Chile: Infrastructure Governance Review*, OECD Publishing, Paris, https://doi.org/10.1787/9789264278875-en. [43]

OECD (2017), *The Governance of Land Use in OECD Countries: Policy Analysis and Recommendations*, OECD Publishing, Paris, https://doi.org/10.1787/9789264268609-en. [20]

OECD (2016), *Making Cities Work for All: Data and Actions for Inclusive Growth*, OECD Publishing, Paris, https://dx.doi.org/10.1787/9789264263260-en. [95]

OECD (2016), *Road Infrastructure, Inclusive Development and Traffic Safety in Korea*, OECD Publishing, Paris, https://doi.org/10.1787/9789264255517-en. [28]

OECD (2015), *Ageing in Cities*, OECD Publishing, Paris, https://doi.org/10.1787/9789264231160-en. [21]

OECD (2015), *Governing the City*, OECD Publishing, Paris, https://doi.org/10.1787/9789264226500-en (accessed on 9 August 2017). [50]

OECD (2015), *OECD Territorial Reviews: Valle de México, Mexico*, OECD Territorial Reviews, OECD Publishing, Paris, https://dx.doi.org/10.1787/9789264245174-en. [51]

OECD (2015), *OECD Urban Policy Reviews: China 2015*, OECD Urban Policy Reviews, OECD Publishing, Paris, https://dx.doi.org/10.1787/9789264230040-en. [92]

OECD (2015), *OECD Urban Policy Reviews: Mexico 2015: Transforming Urban Policy and Housing Finance*, OECD Urban Policy Reviews, OECD Publishing, Paris, https://dx.doi.org/10.1787/9789264227293-en. [90]

OECD (2015), *The Metropolitan Century: Understanding Urbanisation and its Consequences*, OECD Publishing, Paris, https://dx.doi.org/10.1787/9789264228733-en. [1]

OECD (2014), *Compact City Policies: Korea: Towards Sustainable and Inclusive Growth*, OECD Green Growth Studies, OECD Publishing, Paris, https://dx.doi.org/10.1787/9789264225503-en. [79]

OECD (2013), “Vers une croissance plus inclusive de la métropole Aix-Marseille : Une perspective internationale”, OECD, Paris. [30]

OECD (2012), *Compact City Policies: A Comparative Assessment*, OECD Green Growth Studies, OECD Publishing, Paris, https://dx.doi.org/10.1787/9789264167865-en. [3]

OECD (2012), *OECD Urban Policy Reviews, Korea 2012*, OECD Urban Policy Reviews, OECD Publishing, Paris, https://dx.doi.org/10.1787/9789264174153-en. [86]

OECD/European Commission (2020), *Cities in the World: A New Perspective on Urbanisation*, OECD Urban Studies, OECD Publishing, Paris, https://dx.doi.org/10.1787/d0efcbda-en. [2]

Perth, M. and P. Berg (2014), *Hammarby Sjöstad — A New Generation of Sustainable Urban Eco-Districts*, The Nature of Cities, https://www.thenatureofcities.com/2014/02/12/hammarby-sjostad-a-new-generation-of-sustainable-urban-eco-districts/ (accessed on 19 July 2019). [88]

Reid, C. (2018), "Netherlands invests extra €552m to get even more people on bicycles", Forbes, https://www.forbes.com/sites/carltonreid/2018/11/26/dutch-government-invests-extra-e345m-to-get-even-more-people-on-bicycles/#14b8ee123bc6 (accessed on 27 July 2020). [54]

Rode, P. et al. (2014), "Accessibility in cities: Transport and urban form", *NCE Cities Paper 03*, LSE Cities, London School of Economics and Political Science, http://www.lsecities.net (accessed on 9 July 2019). [5]

Rode, P. et al. (2019), *National Transport Policy and Cities: Key Policy Interventions to Drive Compact and Connected Urban Growth*, Coalition for Urban Transitions, London and Washington, http://www.coalitionforurbantransitions.org (accessed on 2 October 2020). [13]

Rodriguez, M. (2017), "Mobility as a Service (#MaaS). How to "plug in". Finland case", Moviliblog, https://blogs.iadb.org/transporte/en/mobility-as-a-service-maas-how-to-plug-in-finland-case/ (accessed on 9 August 2019). [68]

ROPID (n.d.), *Homepage*, http://stary.ropid.cz/info/we-introduce-pid__s219x903. [39]

SEMOVI (2019), *Plan estratégico de género y movilidad 2019*, Secretaría de Movilidad, Mexico City. [73]

Singh, S. (2014), "Women in cars: Overtaking men on the fast lane", Forbes, https://www.forbes.com/sites/sarwantsingh/2014/05/23/women-in-cars-overtaking-men-on-the-fast-lane/#1a72bbaf68d2 (accessed on 4 March 2020). [74]

Straatemeier, T. (2008), "How to plan for regional accessibility?", *Transport Policy*, Vol. 15, pp. 127-137, http://dx.doi.org/10.1016/j.tranpol.2007.10.002. [8]

Taskinen, J. et al. (2016), "City of Turku leads the way towards digitalisation and MaaS in Finland", Intelligent Transport, https://www.intelligenttransport.com/transport-articles/73424/city-turku-transport-digitalisation/ (accessed on 9 August 2019). [69]

TransLink (2013), *Regional Transportation Strategy: Strategic Framework*, TransLink, Vancouver, https://www.translink.ca/-/media/Documents/plans_and_projects/regional_transportation_strategy/rts_strategic_framework_07_31_2013.pdf?la=en&hash=0A459174FB44A8870D00EFCE54124A01078D0698 (accessed on 29 March 2018). [94]

Transport for London (2018), *Cycling Action Plan: Making London the World's Best Big City for Cycling*, Transport for London, London, http://content.tfl.gov.uk/cycling-action-plan.pdf (accessed on 3 September 2019). [44]

UITP (2018), "Public transport as an instrument for urban regeneration", UITP, Brussels, https://www.uitp.org/sites/default/files/cck-focus-papers-files/Policy%20Brief%20-%20PT%20and%20Urban%20Regeneration-BAT-WEB-300DPI.pdf (accessed on 24 April 2019). [85]

Veryard, D. and S. Perkins (2017), "Integrating Urban Public Transport Systems and Cycling: Summary and Conclusions of the ITF Roundtable on Integrated and Sustainable Urban Transport 24-25 April 2017, Tokyo", ITF, Paris, http://www.itf-oecd.org (accessed on 29 July 2020). [36]

World Bank (2015), "Integrated public transport systems make travel easier and more affordable", World Bank, Washington, DC, https://www.worldbank.org/en/news/press-release/2015/04/07/integrated-public-transport-systems-make-travel-easier-and-more-affordable (accessed on 6 August 2019). [35]

Yanocha, D. (2019), "The electric assist: Leveraging e-bikes and e-scooters for more liveable cities", TIDP. [52]

ZTM (n.d.), *About ZTM - Information*, Zarząd Transportu Miejskiego, https://www.ztm.waw.pl/?c=138&l=2 (accessed on 10 September 2019). [33]

Notes

[1] High-income households during 1980-2000 in the United States have demonstrated higher sensitivity to the supply of local amenities: cities where the supply of local amenities grew the most are also cities where the share of highly educated individuals rose fastest (Diamond, 2016[97]).

[2] Moretti (2012[98]) provides a personal example: "Take the Mission District, the neighbourhood of San Francisco where I live. It is one of the areas of the city that has been most affected by the influx of college educated high-tech professionals. Since it is close to the freeway, many workers in Silicon Valley who prefer an urban lifestyle end up here. Remarkably, the people who are benefiting most from this influx of high-tech workers are the largely Latino home owners who have been selling their property to the newcomers – people like the Mexican American couple who owned a nice two-story Victorian near my house that had been in the family for decades. They decided to sell it for $950,000 and move to the suburbs, where they could buy a similar sized house for half the price and live off the balance."

[3] Land value capture can be a means to achieve a more equitable distribution of the gains associated with transport infrastructure improvements. By allowing public authorities to recoup part of the investment costs by partially shifting the burden on private subjects benefitting from transport infrastructure improvements through the increase in land values (i.e. landowners and private developers), land value capture creates the spending capacity to subsidise affordable housing in the proximity of the new infrastructure (see Chapter 2).

[4] Rapid transit may be understood as the high-quality transport service that delivers fast, comfortable and cost-effective services. The service could be provided by Bus-Rapid Transit Systems (BRT), a system of railways (metro, trams, suburban trains) used for local transit in a metropolitan area. The characteristic is that they use a rapid transit line underground (metro), at street level or even above the ground.

[5] Growth strategies aimed at reducing unemployment in cities are a clear example of how inclusiveness and growth objectives can be successfully combined (OECD, 2016[95]).

[6] They also calculate a negative spill-over on the job-finding rate in central London, where job seekers would suffer from increased competition from Stratford.

[7] For further information, see Mustel Group, https://mustelgroup.com/covid-19-the-future-of-transit-in-metro-vancouver-uncertain/.

[8] For further information, see Diario ABC Madrid, https://www.abc.es/espana/madrid/abci-10-por-ciento-madrilenos-dejara-transporte-publico-para-pasarse-coche-privado-crisis-covid-19-202006031305_noticia.html.

[9] For further information, see https://www.railwaypro.com/wp/warsaw-makes-progress-public-transport-development/.

[10] For further information, see UNEP, https://www.unenvironment.org/resources/annual-report/share-road-programme-annual-report-2018.

[11] For further information, see https://www.eleconomista.es/nacional/noticias/10582841/06/20/La-demanda-de-bicicletas-aumenta-un-260-durante-mayo-con-vistas-a-cambiar-el-modelo-de-transporte-en-Espana.html.

[12] For further information, see BiciMAD, https://www.bicimad.com/

[13] For further information, see Shared Micromobility in the US 2018, https://nacto.org/shared-micromobility-2018/.

[14] The government of British Columbia accompanied the introduction of carbon taxation with the commitment by the state government to redistribute the carbon tax proceeds in the form of business tax cuts and tax credits, personal income tax cuts (targeted at lower-income categories), low-income tax credits, reductions in property taxes and even a Climate Action Tax Credit for every citizen (Carbon Pricing Leadership Coalition, 2016[96]).

[15] Despite the similarities, car sharing therefore differs from services through which private individuals rent their cars or motorcycles to other private individuals, including for long durations (e.g. Drivy, SocialCar, etc.). It also differs from carpooling, through which a rider and car owner offers the possibility to others of joining him/her on a given trip in exchange for the reimbursement of trip-related expenses exclusively, thus without the intention of profiting from it.

[16] Among the measures implemented are the elimination of registration fee, value added tax (VAT) and road tolls on newly sold EVs.

[17] Recent asymmetric technological advancements put the price gap between electric and internal combustion engine vehicles at the risk of opening even further, as happened, for instance, when more cost-effective shale gas extraction methods started becoming available in the most recent years.

[18] Data refers to 2018 and is available at https://www.fhwa.dot.gov/policyinformation/statistics/2018/dl220.cfm (accessed 17 March 2020).

[19] For further information, see "Sensorial accessibility", https://www.ratp.fr/en/accessibility/sensorial-accessibility.

[20] For further information, see https://www.metromadrid.es/en/travel-in-the-metro/card-types.

[21] For further information, see https://tfl.gov.uk/corporate/about-tfl/corporate-and-social-responsibility/equality-and-inclusion.

[22] Urban density is the measure of an urban unit of interest (e.g. population, employment and housing) per area unit (e.g. block, neighbourhood, city, metropolitan area and nation). The three most common measures of density are population (i.e. population per unit area), built-up area (i.e. buildings or urban land cover per unit area) and employment density (i.e. jobs per unit area) (IPCC, 2014, p. 952[14]).

[23] For further information, see https://www.jhsph.edu/news/news-releases/2020/urban-density-not-linked-to-higher-coronavirus-infection-rates-and-is-linked-to-lower-covid-19-death-rates.html.

[24] For further information, see www.thenatureofcities.com/2014/02/12/hammarby-sjostad-a-new-generation-of-sustainable-urban-eco-districts/.

2 Planning and governance for accessible cities

This chapter proposes some actions cities may undertake to improve planning and governance arrangements to build accessible cities. It argues that fostering urban accessibility requires a holistic planning approach, a sound institutional framework, reliable sources of funding, enhanced governmental capacity (staff) and strong community engagement. The chapter starts with an exploration of how cities organise their planning framework for accessibility. It then continues with a discussion on the different governance arrangements needed to promote and support urban accessibility policies. The discussion focuses on how cities adapt their institutional framework to improve transport planning and ensure they have access to potential sources of funding to implement those plans. The chapter highlights the need for improving governments' need for qualified staff and access to reliable data. It concludes with a discussion on how community engagement can be better pursued to enhanced urban accessibility.

Key messages

Enhancing urban accessibility faces a number of barriers linked to the level of socio-economic development and capacity of the public sector in each country and city. The COVID-19 pandemic may be both a triggering force for urban accessibility but also a barrier as recovery measures, such as a wider use of private cars, may undermine efforts to promote accessible cities. The challenge for countries and cities is to remain on track in pursuing compactness, inclusiveness, sustainability and accessibility while designing policies to "build back better" after the current pandemic.

Key takeaways for national and subnational policymakers are:

- Enhancing accessibility requires a holistic planning approach that links social, economic and environmental aspects to ensure that planning of the city's movement and traffic contributes to building accessible and attractive cities.
- A way to promote urban accessibility through the planning framework is by building "transit-oriented communities" (TOCs). TOCs intend to maximise access to transit as a key organising principle and acknowledge mobility as an integral part of the urban fabric. TOCs require designing and planning high-density, mixed-use, human-scale development around frequent transit stops and stations.
- Promoting accessibility is a way of contributing to environmental goals as it can reduce the need for mobility or make mobility more efficient and thus reduce emissions. Reducing travel demand by improving accessibility, facilitating the use of high-occupancy mobility and encouraging active mobility (walking and cycling) can help reduce CO_2 emissions from urban transport.
- Planning for accessibility requires cross-cutting policies and co-ordination across policy areas and levels of government to reduce transaction costs. For that purpose, having one agency (normally at the metropolitan level) that facilitates the planning and implementation of transport strategy is a way to advance accessibility goals and improve technical and financial capacities.
- The success of any transport and accessibility strategy depends on how intergovernmental relations are structured. There should be a coherent allocation of responsibilities across levels of government based on multiyear strategic planning.
- Countries and cities need to explore different sources of funding for transport strategies that promote accessibility. Some alternatives include:
    - Devolving or granting more financial powers to cities, which could allow them to manage their own growth.
    - Developing land value capture mechanisms to fund further developments.
    - Creating public partnerships for funding transport investments.
    - Involving the private sector in funding public transport infrastructure.
    - Adopting a medium-term budget framework for transport investment.
- Cities need to improve their capacity for accessibility through investing in a highly skilled workforce and developing the capacity for data collection and *ex post* assessment to build expertise.
- Promoting dialogue with and engagement of citizens and a wider set of stakeholders is a way to harness the knowledge of citizens. Involving all levels of government, customers and industry in discussing critical transport problems and together finding innovative solutions is a way to foster a high level of collaboration and decision-making.

Planning for accessibility in cities

The barriers to enhancing accessibility

Changing the urban transport model and promoting accessibility faces some barriers or resistance in all cities. Researchers argue that there is a sparsity of knowledge about accessibility and a disconnect between policymaking and accessibility outcomes; thus, research mainly analyses topics such as land use, housing and transport dissociated from one another (Duranton and Guerra, 2016[1]).

Despite large investments in public transport infrastructure and services in many cities, cars remain the dominant urban transport mode. Although the economic, social and environmental case for promoting public transit over the use of private cars is strong, industry sectors, such as the car industry, construction and real estate, which are still highly dependent on the traditional urbanisation model and are proving resistant to change (Rode et al., 2014[2]). For instance, the Prague metropolitan area in the Czech Republic continues to pursue a car-friendly approach and is ranked 26th (out of 30) in the European Green City Index in the transport category. In contrast to the high level of public transport use within the city of Prague, cross-border commuters rely predominantly on cars. The lack of mobility options to connect the city and the metropolitan region through public transport has led to an increase in car ownership and traffic in recent years (Lukeš, Kotek and Růžička, 2014[3]). In Spain, the total number of trips during a weekday in the Madrid region is 12.9 million of which approximately 70% are made by mechanised modes (private vehicle and public transport) and 30% by walking (Velasco, 2016[4]). These data show that the use of the private car is still the main means of transport in the metropolitan zone. However, a large percentage of citizens prefer walking. In some areas outside the city of Madrid, the use of the car may reach 50% as transport coverage is not extensive.

COVID-19 is undermining the efforts to reduce car use. Countries are issuing measures to reactivate the economy after the pandemic. However, in some cases, they go in reverse to previous policies such as reducing the use of private cars in favour of public transport. For example, auto sales in China plummeted 45% in March 2020 from a year earlier. The auto industry makes up 10% of the country's gross domestic product (GDP) and most auto plants have restarted and supply chains are being restored. Hence, national and regional governments decided to extend subsidies for new energy vehicles (electric vehicles and plug-in hybrids) by two years.[1] According to this measure, owners of new energy vehicles will receive at least CNY 10 000 (approximately USD 1 400) in tax breaks per vehicle. The programme was supposed to expire at the end of 2020 but the government seeks to boost economic recovery by supporting demand. Beijing is considering issuing 100 000 more license plates for new energy vehicles alone. Local authorities expect that this measure will represent more than CNY 20 billion (approximately USD 2.9 billion) in auto sales. The city of Guangzhou plans to issue more than 10 000 license plates a month. Nine cities have adopted separate subsidies for vehicle purchase. In Guangzhou, home to several domestic and foreign auto plants, authorities have allocated CNY 450 million (approximately USD 67 million) for the programme.[2]

Urban areas with a low density and car-oriented legacy face high costs to switch to high-density public transit-oriented areas. Urban infrastructure may not be adequate to support high levels of density and public transport would need to be upgraded to provide better services to a larger number of passengers. In Vancouver, the transport authority has given priority to upgrading the existent infrastructure to improve the efficiency of the transport network in the context of a growing number of passengers. In Mexico City, the Strategic Mobility Plan 2019 aims at improving the existing infrastructure and services to reduce commuting time, improve safety and make freight transport more efficient. Moreover, higher-income households in cities in developing countries still prefer to own a car and have a lifestyle in the suburbs due to a lack of viable transport options and this is also regarded as a way to maintain their status and safety. In some cities with a Soviet past, citizens opted to use private transport as soon as there was a change in the political regime and despite having a relatively extensive public transport network. In Almaty, Kazakhstan, for instance, the number of private vehicles increased from 200 500 in 2001 to 460 000 in

2011 (OECD, 2017[5]). For many residents, owning a car represents a new status and local authorities planned for car-oriented infrastructure. The problem is that the public transport system characterised by an extensive network of buses, trolleybuses and trams was neglected. Expanding and modernising Almaty's transport system is proving a considerable logistical, planning, administrative and financial challenge for local authorities with the result that Almaty's transport network is now old, unsafe, inadequate and a source of pollution.

The lack of active mobility options (e.g. cycling) may be a hindrance for promoting accessibility. In several cities, environmentally friendly mobility options are still largely underdeveloped and thus the levels of cycling are rather low (i.e. Bucharest, Prague, Rome, Tallinn). Cycling is still not part of people's culture in many European cities. Only in Amsterdam, Copenhagen and Groningen does cycling reach more than 50% of the modal share but in the large majority of cities, it represents no more than 10% (EC/UN-Habitat, 2016[6]). In Mexico City, the cycling infrastructure, which has seen progress over the last years, is still scarce, disconnected from the transport network and concentrated in central areas which limits the potential for bicycle use for short and medium distances (SEMOVI, 2019[7]). In other cases, cities need to improve the infrastructure to incentivise walking. In the city of Surrey, Metro Vancouver, sidewalks are missing in many areas with single-family homes.

Cities also face institutional and process barriers to switch the urban transport paradigm (Rode et al., 2014[2]). For instance, a silo approach to urban development still prevails in many cities, disconnecting transport, housing, land use and environmental policies from one another. Cities' master plans are composed of different sections: utilities, healthcare, transport, housing, etc. However, there is no cross-cutting analysis of the main urban priorities of cities and how each sector is expected to help achieve them. Accessibility planning is a cross-sectoral domain and requires local authorities to change their traditional approach to planning. Cities may require planning not by sector but by broader objectives such as equality, inclusiveness, accessibility, safety, etc.

In cities in developing countries, there is a lack of professional personnel specialised in urban transport and planning in general. This is an obstacle to the formation and development of a transport strategy, in line with housing policies, for instance, and the adoption of effective management tools for urban transport. Moreover, promoting accessibility requires working with the existing urban form and flows of the city; the problem is that it is not always possible to change the existing urban form.

Fragmented governance and the lack of co-ordination mechanisms between national and local governments for urban development and accessibility are two very common barriers, mostly in cities in developing countries (Trejo Nieto, Niño Amezquita and Vasquez, 2018[8]). For example, in Latin American cities, it is common to find political-administrative fragmentation and policy implementation resides with individual autonomous local authorities. This represents an obstacle for urban planning and accessibility planning. This fragmentation constrains not only planning but also the joint investment in urban transport infrastructure. There are no mechanisms for local governments to invest together in critical infrastructure. Mexico's reform to guidelines for the operation of metropolitan funds is a promising initiative to overcome the fragmented nature of metropolitan areas to support their joint investment in urban infrastructure such as urban transport.[3]

Accessibility requires a holistic planning approach

Enhancing accessibility requires a holistic planning approach that links social, economic and environmental aspects. The aim is to ensure that planning of the city's movement and traffic contributes to building accessible and attractive cities (City of Malmö, 2016[9]; Gil Solá, Vilhelmson and Larsson, 2018[10]). The reason is that if citizens are going to have access to services distributed in a geographic area, then several contexts must systematically be adapted to different requirements. For instance, trips must run smoothly for people with different needs (i.e. the elderly, children, handicapped people, etc). This implies that accessibility planning involves trade-offs between interests, groups of citizens and planning departments.

By taking a holistic approach to planning, cities can use the movement of people and public transport to achieve bigger objectives such as sustainability, equity, inclusiveness and growth. A city consists of many different components and one of the most important ones is people and how they move within, to and from the city. For the city of Gothenburg, Sweden, transport is a means of achieving a functioning and attractive city (City of Gothenburg, 2014[11]). The transport strategy, therefore, needs to be developed in an integrated process with a development planning strategy and environmental strategy. Altogether, these documents constitute an important part of a city's land use with the aim of specifying the objectives and strategies of the comprehensive plan (Figure 2.1).

Figure 2.1. Gothenburg's transport strategy within the planning framework

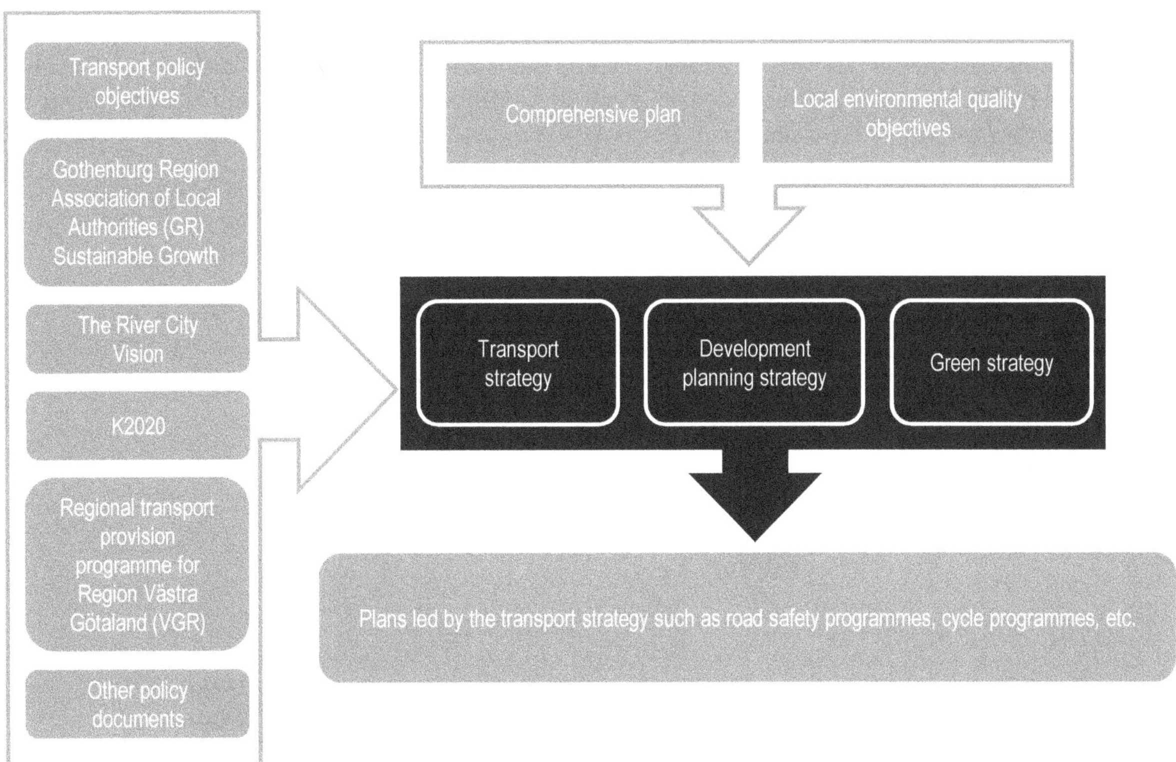

Source: Elaborated based on City of Gothenburg (2014[11]), *Gothenburg 2035 - Transport Strategy for a Close-Knit City*, https://goteborg.se/wps/wcm/connect/6c603463-f0b8-4fc9-9cd4-c1e934b41969/Trafikstrategi_eng_140821_web.pdf?MOD=AJPERES (accessed on 16 July 2019).

While the transport strategy should recognise the geographical, economic and social challenges of a city, it should also seek to preserve resources, such as land. However, city planning authorities need to consider that there is no universal rule or attribution of how land should be used. Cities will continue growing and choices have to be made of where that growth should take place. Planners need to balance the trade-offs of resource preservation and protection of natural resources based on the local context and development objectives of the city.

Transport planning should be target-led rather than prediction-based (City of Gothenburg, 2014[11]). In other words, there should be realistic targets to achieve based on the local needs and the specific socio-economic context. The transport strategy should avoid forecasts as they are not useful for measuring progress. In Australia, for example, the New South Wales (NSW) transport strategy from 2016 sets a vision for the next 40 years on how transport can help build a productive economy, liveable communities and sustainable society (Box 2.1).

In Metro Vancouver, Canada, the transport authority, TransLink, issues a 10-year investment plan that outlines the strategic initiatives, transportation programmes and services it plans to deliver over the period. These include: level of services to be provided; major capital projects and key initiatives, estimated expenditures, estimated revenues and estimated borrowing. These plans set the annual transportation investments and actions and are in line with the Regional Transportation Strategy.

Box 2.1. Transport strategies support regional development goals

Malmö's accessibility vision

The city of Malmö, Sweden, has adopted its Sustainable Urban Mobility Plan to create a more accessible city. It sets how the traffic system and urban environments can contribute to creating an accessible city for a greater number of people. It takes the view that better accessibility and increased sustainable mobility give more people access to more qualitative urban environments contributing to the development of the city. Its vision is:

> *Walking, cycling and public transport are the first choice for all who work, live or visit in Malmö. These travel choices, together with efficient and environmentally friendly freight and car traffic, are the basis of the transport system in our dense, sustainable city – a transport system designed for the city, and for its people.*

The plans acknowledges that the major change to create a more balanced modal split in a growing city is to increase the share of cycling and public transport over car traffic. This increases the opportunities for a more socially, environmentally and economically sustainable city. The objectives for 2030 are shown in the figure below:

Figure 2.2. Malmö's objectives for inhabitants' trips

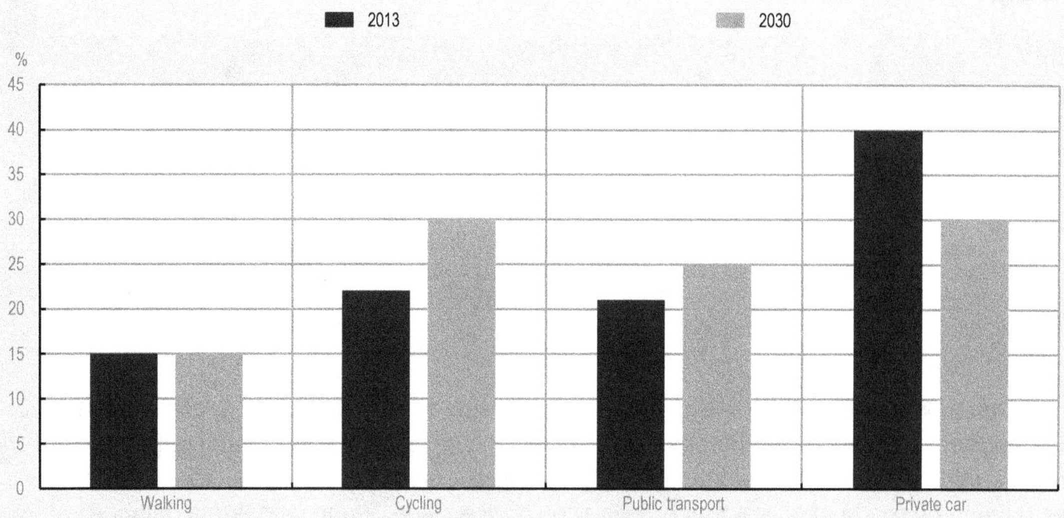

2013 2030

%

45 40 35 30 25 20 15 10 5 0

Walking Cycling Public transport Private car

The city does not seek to increase commuting but to make commuting more economically, socially and environmentally sustainable. The city's objectives for 2030 are:

Figure 2.3. Malmö's objectives for commuting to the city

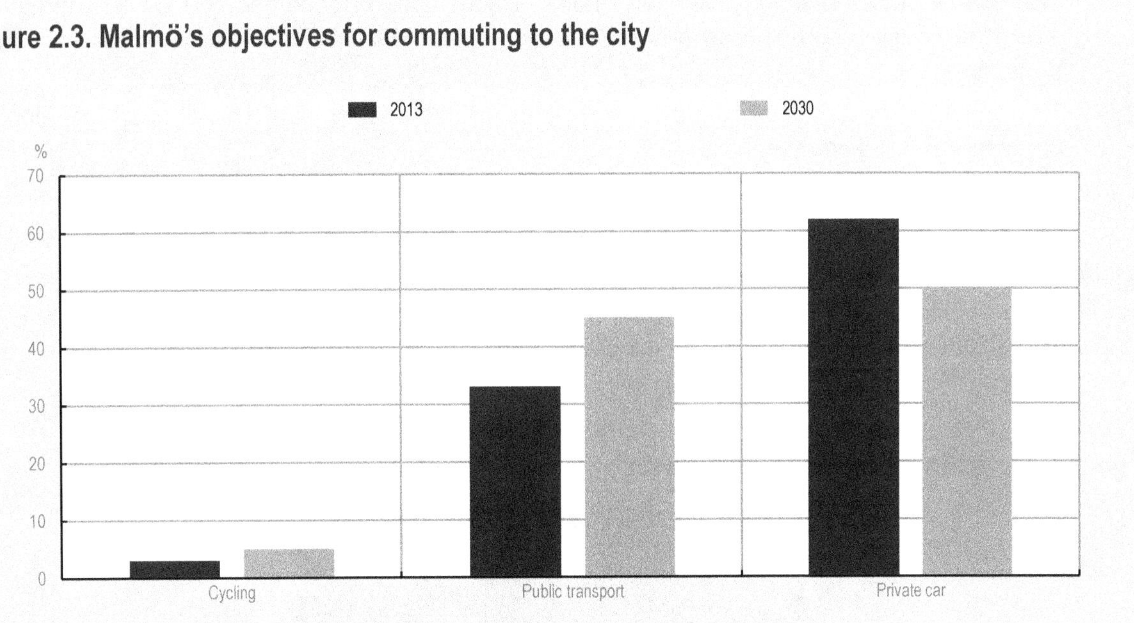

Sydney's Future Transport Strategy 2056

The New South Wales (NSW) Future Transport Strategy 2056 is a suite of strategies and plans for transport developed by the regional government in co-ordination with the Greater Sydney Commission. This document sets the 40-year vision, directions and outcomes framework for customer mobility in NSW, which is expected to guide transport investment over the long term and be delivered through a series of supporting plans. The strategy acknowledges transport as an enabler of economic and social activity and a contributor to long-term economic, social and environmental outcomes. The vision builds on six outcomes: customer-focused, successful places, a strong economy, safety and performance, accessible services and sustainability. Each of these outcomes was set to guide investment, policy and reform and service provision. The strategy envisions Greater Sydney, a metropolis of 3 cities, as a place where people can access jobs, education and services within 30 minutes by public or active (walking and cycling) transport.

Source: City of Malmö (2016[9]), *Sustainable Urban Mobility Plan: Creating a More Sustainable Malmö*, https://malmo.se/download/18.16ac037b154961d0287384d/1491301288704/Sustainable+urban+mobility+plan%28TROMP%29_ENG.pdf (accessed on 16 July 2019); NSW Government (2018[12]), *Future Transport Strategy 2056*, https://future.transport.nsw.gov.au/sites/default/files/media/documents/2018/Future_Transport_2056_Strategy.pdf.

The planning process requires clear policies at all levels of government with a specific target for mode share and enhanced environmental standards. The experience of London, United Kingdom (UK), and Vancouver suggests that securing funding for transport from increased land values and working with stakeholders and communities in and outside the city is essential for delivering sustainable growth. Some of the aspects that would contribute to getting the planning process right, according to the experience of London (Greater London Authority, 2018[13]), are:

- The development of mechanisms for co-ordinating planning and investment along transport growth corridors.
- The development of opportunity area planning frameworks[4] with ambitious mode shares for walking, cycling and public transport. This requires maximising the investment in transport infrastructure.

- The use of public sector funding for smaller-scale transport schemes that could contribute to unlocking housing construction and job creation, and leverage funding from other sources for transport.
- The inclusion of sustainable growth principles in the assessment of transport development proposals and requirements.
- Ensure that the transport plans for the transport authority encourage efficient and sustainable travel.

Figure 2.4 shows London's strategy to foster "good growth". It reveals that the city's strategy to enhance and increase public transport is based on land use planning. Transport services and infrastructure also shape the city by enabling high-density development and liveable neighbourhoods where people want to live and work.

Figure 2.4. London's cycle of "good growth"

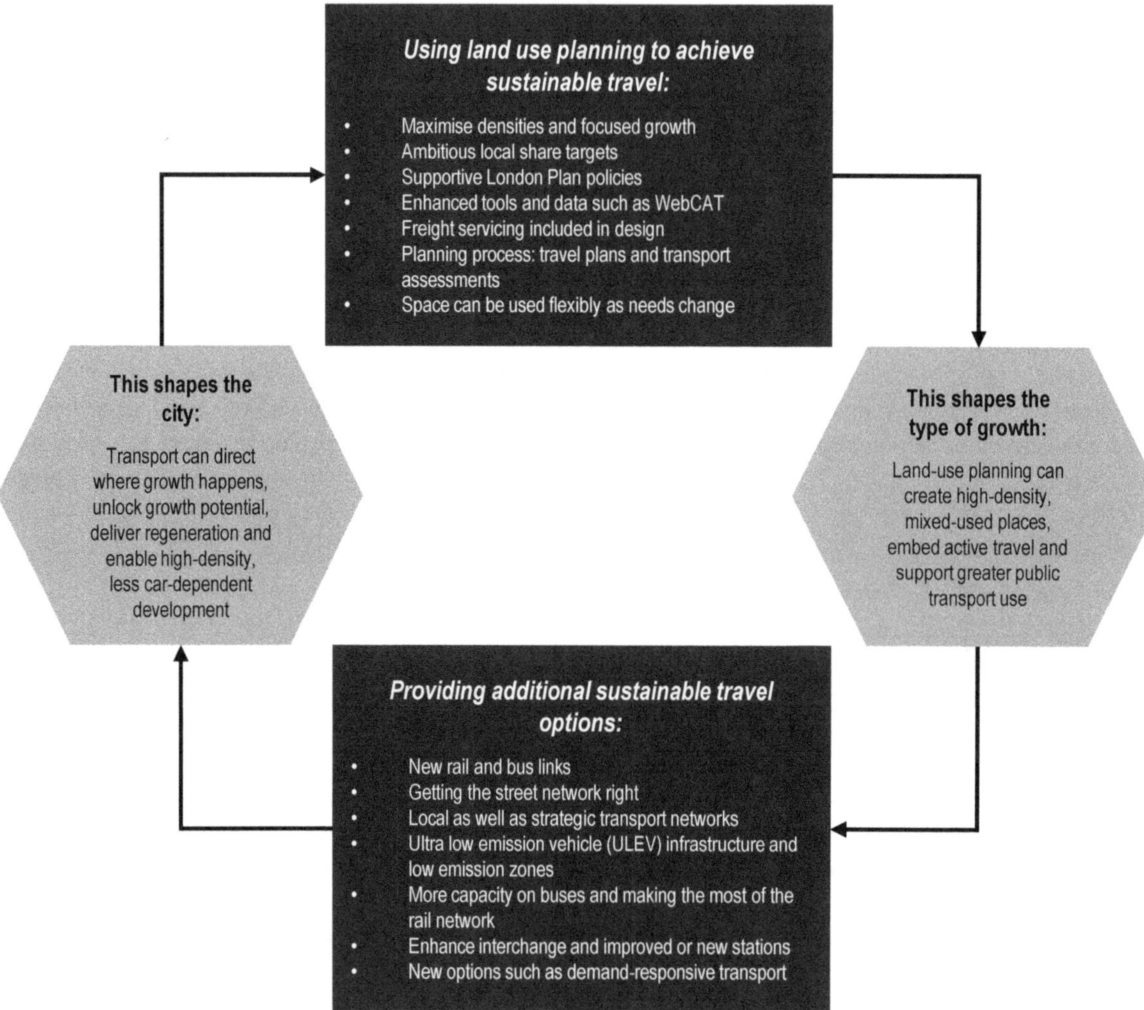

Source: Based on Greater London Authority (2018[13]), *Mayor's Transport Strategy*, http://www.london.gov.uk (accessed on 15 July 2019).

How the planning framework can foster accessibility

In general, countries have a hierarchical system of urban development plans. They provide guidelines for regional and local planning and set priorities for investment based on national goals.

The national planning framework sets guidelines and goals

At the national level, countries have a spatial development policy that contains planning guidelines and outlines the general vision for spatial development. Their purpose is to ensure integrated territorial development, prevent space-social segregation in urban development and, in some cases, set the development planning priorities for their main metropolitan areas.

Some countries have a complex, hierarchical system or urban development plans. In these cases, regional and local development plans and urban strategies should be co-ordinated with national development priorities. National legislation may include provision for the development of transport and related infrastructure and, in several instances, they are built based on inputs from regional and local levels of government. Their provisions tend to be mandatory and should be included in greater detail in the spatial development plans of lower levels of government. The complexity of the national planning framework depends on the country's administrative culture. For example, in Romania, three instruments shape regional development and transport policies at the national level and they are all expected to have their equivalent at the regional level. In principle, this is a good practice as it ensures coherence in the planning approach, priorities for investment and practices, problems may emerge when subnational governments lack the capacity to produce and implement highly detailed plans (Box 2.2). In the Czech Republic, the 2015 Spatial Development Policy (SDP) is at the top of the planning hierarchy framework, contains planning guidelines and delimits development areas as well as the main transport and infrastructure corridors. The SDP does not outline a general vision for spatial development but establishes planning priorities for, among other issues, sustainable development, corridors and areas for transport infrastructure.

Box 2.2. Romania's transport planning framework

In Romania, there are three planning instruments that affect directly or indirectly transport planning in the country:

- **National Spatial Plan** (Law 363, 2006) – transport section. It provides an outline of the main transport sectors that need investment in order to improve the national transport network: motorways, transport networks and other infrastructure projects. It states that the central, county and local public administration authorities have to co-operate to ensure the enforcement of the provisions contained in the plan.
- **Transport General Master Plan**. It was approved in 2016 and represents the general development framework for transportation infrastructure, financing sources and strategy for project implementation. It sets the strategic objectives and the main transport corridors in line with the trans-European strategic objectives for transport infrastructure. It contains a detailed description of envisaged projects for construction. The approval of the plan also represents a conditionality for obtaining funds from the European Union (EU).
- **National Territorial Development Strategy 2035**. Its aim is to ensure a strategic planning integrated framework to guide the national territorial development process. Its mission is to ensure a polycentric development and balance between the need for development and the competitive advantages of the national territory in the European and global contexts.

Source: Ministry of Regional Development and Public Administration of Romania.

Subnational governments operationalise national transport priorities

Subnational levels of government have a critical role to play in planning. In particular, municipal planning has the potential to help manage change and growth in the long term. Municipalities have a wider responsibility to promote economic growth, social well-being and environmental sustainability for their communities in a context of constant change. Managing change in housing demand and how the municipality will respond to future public transport needs are issues that require planning at the local level. The reason is because priorities differ from one municipality to another (and sometimes from one neighbourhood to another) depending on things like natural resource dependency, rate of population increase, etc. A critical point of municipal planning is carrying it out together with citizens and a wide range of stakeholders from the private and social sectors.

A transport strategy is needed to make the most of urbanisation. Cities are growing in terms of residents and economic activity. To manage that growth the transport strategy is key. It can help to reduce the climate impact of the transport sector by giving people more and better travel options, disincentivising the use of private cars. It can also contribute to strengthening the economic competitiveness of a city by offering a vibrant urban life and good business conditions. One of the key advantages of the transport strategy is that it can help cities to set priorities to achieve urban development objectives. The transport strategy states the city's overall focus for planning and decisions on investments and other measures not only in the area of transport but also on other urban-related areas.

Most cities and metropolitan areas, if not all, have a strategy to improve public transport services. The transport strategy is the guiding document for how the transport system of a city is to be developed in order to achieve the mobility and accessibility objectives in the medium and long terms. It states a city's or region's overall focus for planning and decisions on investments on transport. It elaborates the transport elements of the regional development strategy, the comprehensive development plans and other strategic documents (Figure 2.5). It provides guidance to cities and municipalities for achieving and accommodating growth as it supports other urban development areas such as housing, the environment, etc. It may include a provision on, or be the basis for, more specific, concrete documents such as plans on the bus, bicycle, pedestrian systems and land use which are needed to achieve the objectives of the transport strategy. All these elements may be elaborated at the regional but also at the local level depending on the country's governance arrangements. The transport strategy sets the goals that the city wants to achieve regarding well-being, urban environment and urban structure. Generally, these documents should be guided in future planning and budgeting at administrations responsible for urban development and sustainable transport. They are addressed to politicians, officials and planners at all levels of government as well as to inhabitants and private sector parties. Transport strategies differ in their level of sophistication and above all how they are linked to land use and socio-economic development policies.

To promote accessibility, cities require a new approach to transport investment and development. Traditionally, cities adopt a transit-oriented development (TOD) approach to achieve sustainable development. TOD is considered an effective way of concentrating growth on brownfield sites (i.e. areas already developed) while generating and attracting ridership to shift mode shares towards public transport. TODs are site-specific projects in close proximity to rapid transit stations. Benefits of TOD include: agglomeration effects boosting a city's competitiveness (doubling job density increases economic productivity by 5%-10%); making cities more liveable; increasing real estate value; cities capturing part of the increase in real estate value to finance additional transit investments (e.g. in Hong Kong, the People's Republic of China [China hereafter], land value capture brought in approximately HKD 140 billion (USD 18 billion) between 1980 and 2005 and unlocked land for 600 000 public housing units); enhancing job opportunities and services for residents; reducing emissions; and helping to enhance resilience to disasters (Salat and Ollivier, 2017[14]).[5] However, TOD cannot be implemented in the same way in all places. The specific characteristics of every place and project need to be assessed to determine the viability of the project (Box 2.3).

Figure 2.5. Relationship between regional growth strategies and transport planning across levels of government

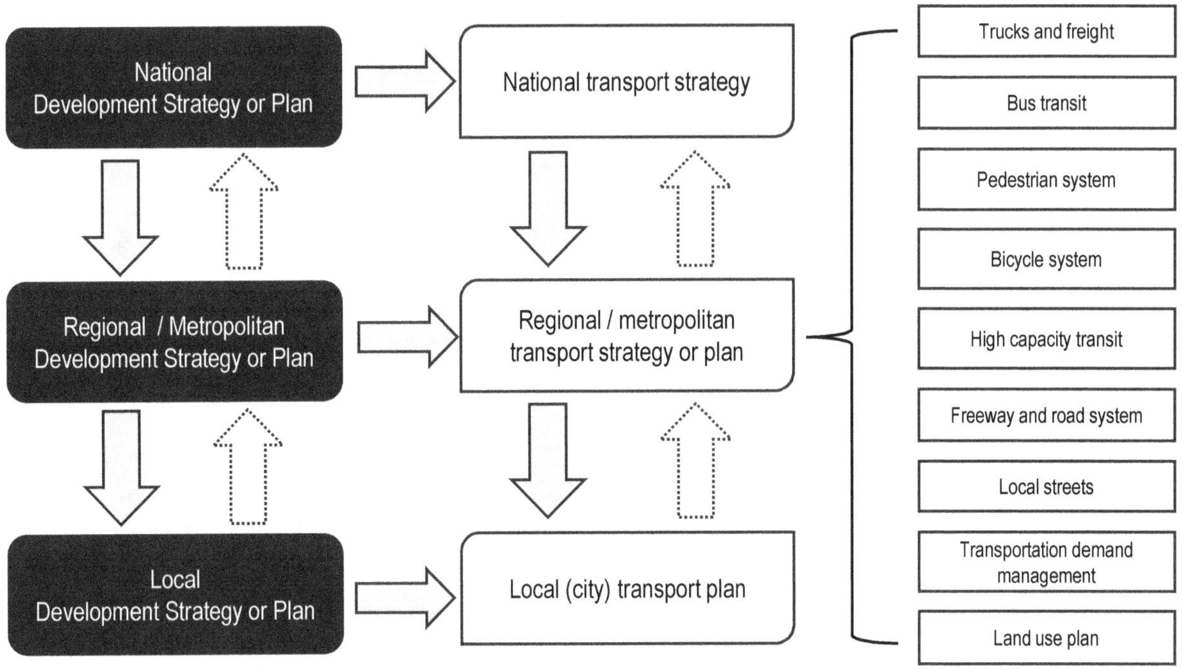

From transit-oriented development to transit-oriented communities

Box 2.3. Assessing the three values (3V) of transit-oriented development

Since TOD cannot be implemented uniformly across an entire city due to varying densities, the World Bank has developed a framework for guiding TOD plans by simultaneously assessing the "three values" (3V) of transit stations and surrounding areas:

- The **node value** – which refers to the importance of a station in the public transit network based on passenger traffic, connections with other transport modes and centrality within the network.
- The **place value** – which assesses the quality and attractiveness of the area around the station. It includes factors such as the diversity of land use, the availability of essential services, the proportion of amenities that can be accessed by active mobility, pedestrian accessibility and the size of urban blocks around stations.
- The **market potential value** – which refers to the unrealised market value of station areas. It looks at the major variables that influence the demand for land (i.e. current and future number of jobs in the vicinity of the station) as well as the supply (i.e. amount of developable land).

Source: Salat, S. and G. Ollivier (2017[14]), *Transforming the Urban Space through Transit-Oriented Development: The 3V Approach*, https://openknowledge.worldbank.org/handle/10986/26405 (accessed on 10 September 2019).

However, some metropolitan areas such as Vancouver prefer to focus on transit-oriented communities (TOCs) which refer to places that, by design, allow people to drive less and walk, cycle and take public transport more often. It promotes higher-density, mixed-use, human-scale development around frequent transit stops and stations. The main difference with TODs is that TOCs are places that take access to and support for transit into account when planning and designing at a neighbourhood, corridor, municipal or regional scale. This is a planning concept that includes land use planning and community development policies that intend to maximise access to transit as a key to organising principle and acknowledge mobility as an integral part of the urban fabric. By connecting communities, destinations and amenities through improved access to transit, TOCs promote walkable and bikeable communities that accommodate healthier and active lifestyles, improve access to jobs and economic opportunities, and reduce greenhouse gas (GHG) emissions. TOCs may be an approach other OECD cities may be interested in exploring to improve accessibility. In fact, TOCs is a planning approach that is in line with the OECD Principles on Urban Policy, which suggest the need to adapt policy action to the place where people live and work. This can be done by adapting development strategies and public service delivery to the diversity of urban scales, ranging from neighbourhoods all the way to megacities and megaregions (OECD, 2019[15]).

One potential problem, however, is that TOCs can also create equity challenges. Indeed, TOCs can disproportionately favour individuals and families who are able to pay the extra premium to live in valuable real estate proximate to rapid transit. Subsequently, lower-income households have limited locational choices and they often get pushed further away from better-served transit areas, resulting in less equitable transit access for the less affluent (Ngo, 2012[16]). This could be attenuated, at least in part, by providing transport options for all members of the community and reducing households transport costs through less driving and potentially lower automobile ownership rates.

The regional development/growth strategy sets investment priorities

Accessibility requires planning at the regional and local levels. Regions or metropolitan areas normally have a development/growth strategy and a transport strategy in line with national development goals. The regional development/growth strategy is a guiding document for the development of new local residential and employment growth targets and updates local comprehensive plans. In general, regions and metro areas use the regional development or regional growth strategy to: i) determine investment priorities; ii) promote infill and redevelopment within urban areas to create more compact, walkable and transit-friendly communities; and iii) set the long-term development vision for regional growth and a clear pathway for ensuring that growth benefits every member of the community. The goals are generally linked to the city's vision and sustainable development goals and act as support for all city planning and urban development. In the Czech Republic, Prague's 2016 Strategic Plan determines the primary direction for development in the medium and long term (10-15 years) and sets out the city's social and economic objectives and priorities. It offers diagnoses of the major challenges facing the city and the critical areas for action and investment across a wide range of policy areas – from education to transportation and land use planning. In Krakow, Poland, the local development strategy highlights the investment priorities in transport investment in accordance with local needs, the national development priorities stated in the Strategy for Responsible Development (SRD) and EU directives (Krakow City, 2017[17]).

In the Canadian Metro Vancouver Regional District for instance, the regional growth strategy operates in co-ordination with the Regional Transportation Strategy. Together, these two documents serve as the underpinning for the definition of 10-year investment plans as well as the municipal transportation and economic development plans (Box 2.4).

Some cities and metro regions lack a regional growth or development strategy although it is legally possible for them to have one. The lack of a strategy makes it difficult to co-ordinate economic, land use, transport, housing and environment policies at the regional level as urban and regional planning are limited to the boundaries of the municipalities. This is the case of the Spanish Madrid region (*Comunidad Autónoma de*

Madrid, CAM) which lacks a formal regional development strategy, with each municipality conducting its own planning individually without a co-ordinated vision. The regional authority (CAM) ensures that each of the 179 municipalities in the region follows the legal process but there is little discussion on their regional implications.

Box 2.4. Metro Vancouver's Regional Growth Strategy

Metro Vancouver 2040: Shaping Our Future is the Regional Growth Strategy (RGS), a high-level land use plan which contains the region's goals, actions and strategies. It focuses on land use policies to guide development – mostly around Frequent Transit Development Areas (FTDA) – and to support the efficient provision of transport, regional infrastructure and community services, as well as to protect air quality and reduce GHG emissions. The RGS is one plan among a suite of interconnected management plans developed around Metro Vancouver's Sustainability Framework, for instance, Metro Vancouver's Integrated Air Quality and Greenhouse Gas Management Plan; TransLink's Regional Transportation Strategy; and the Regional Transportation Investment Vision by the Mayors' Council on Regional Transportation. The RGS and the Regional Transportation Strategy are mutually reinforcing.

Source: Mayors'Council on Regional Transportation (2017[18]), *Regional Transportation Investments - A Vision for Metro Vancouver*, https://tenyearvision.translink.ca/downloads/10%20Year%20Vision%20for%20Metro%20Vancouver (accessed on 29 March 2018).

Regions may also have specific transport-related plans aimed at co-ordinating transport investment and planning among their constituent municipalities. For instance, the Madrid region has a Strategic Sustainable Mobility Plan (SSMP) that co-ordinates the transport efforts of the different municipalities and presents the vision of what public transport should be in the medium term. In turn, each of the region's municipalities has a Sustainable Urban Mobility Plan (PMUS), a strategic plan designed to meet the mobility needs of people and businesses in cities and their surrounding areas. The PMUS aim to ensure the quality of the environment, urban competitiveness, safety and universal access to transport. They serve as an instrument to co-ordinate the different departments within the local administration and guide infrastructure development. They define priorities, actions, future scenarios, as well as the necessary conditions for implementation.

The organisation of regional planning may be as complex as the governance structure and the level of decentralisation in each country. There is no rule or best practice on how many plans, to what level of detail nor what functions regions should have regarding transport. Most of the time, the problem lies in the capacity of the regions to implement those plans. It may be argued that the main purpose of the regional/metropolitan plans for growth and transport is to co-ordinate investment across the different municipalities within the region/metropolitan area. However, that also depends on the governance arrangements of every country. For instance, Prague, Czech Republic, has the status of a region and is surrounded by another region, the Central Bohemian Region. Prague's transport plans and land use plans are mandatory for the municipalities within the city of Prague and for some in the Central Bohemian Region. The rest of the municipalities must have their own plans co-ordinated by the authority of the Central Bohemian Region. In contrast, in the Metro Vancouver Regional District, the regional growth strategy and transport plans apply to all municipalities in the region even though every municipality is responsible for its own transport plan.

Municipal planning operationalises national and regional plans

Municipalities in metropolitan areas typically have to develop their own development and transport plans even if there is a general plan for the metropolitan area. In most countries, national and provincial laws require municipalities to develop one or more plans for the city's social, economic and physical future. These plans must set a general vision for the city and be in line with the regional development strategies, which in turn are co-ordinated with national priorities. Cites could have a comprehensive transport strategy in addition to that of the regional or municipal level. In the Stockholm City Plan, for instance, the goals of the city plan show how local authorities envision and intend to pursue greater accessibility in the city but, perhaps more importantly, for what purpose.

Box 2.5. Stockholm's planning goals

The overarching city planning goal of Stockholm, Sweden, is to be a city for everyone, with dense and cohesive urban environments in which buildings and green spaces work together, enabling the creation of good living environments. This generic goal is supported by four specific goals:

- ***A growing city*** – attracting people, companies and visitors from across the world. A rapid rate of urban development is to guarantee homes and public services for everyone. Good accessibility is to give people and companies everything they need to develop and grow.
- ***A cohesive city*** – where moving between different areas and visiting new places comes naturally. People with different backgrounds must be able to encounter each other as they go about their daily lives and the city's many urban settings, with all of its different features, must be accessible to all of the city's residents.
- ***Good public spaces*** – the city is to have many, diverse neighbourhoods with strong identities and flourishing local centres. Every part of the city must offer a good environment in which to live, with good access to the benefits of urban living and well-designed, safe public spaces encouraging participation and engagement in local community life.
- ***A climate-smart resilient city*** – in which efficient land use and transport efficient layout foster greater accessibility, a lower climate impact and limited consumption of resources. The structure of the city and its technical systems must be highly functional and resilient, enabling the city to cope with climate change and other stress factors.

Source: City of Stockholm (n.d.[19]), *Stockholm City Plan*, https://vaxer.stockholm/globalassets/tema/oversiktplan-ny_light/english_stockholm_city_plan.pdf (accessed on 12 July 2019).

In Canada, the province of British Columbia requires the municipalities that form the Metropolitan Vancouver Regional District to develop their own official community plans (OCPs). The OCP is a long-term future community planning vision describing the kind of community into which the city wishes to evolve. It constitutes a guiding document for the city council (the legislative body of the municipal government) in future decision-making, ranging from short- to long-term investments, programming and land use changes and provides a broad framework for managing change, including policies to address related needs for amenities, services and infrastructure. OCPs must be in line with the RGS and, in general, specify how they will contribute to the achievement of RGS goals. OCPs are at the top of the hierarchy of land use plans and normally include more specific area and neighbourhood plans. If there is a conflict between the OCP and the area plan, the area plan takes precedence over the citywide policies. Local councils are not obliged to strictly implement the policies of OCPs – the plans may be amended from time to time – but the important requirement is that every amendment must go through a public consultation process that has to include a formal public hearing.

The city of Madrid has a comprehensive planning framework for mobility. Its overarching plan, the Sustainable Urban Mobility Plan (*Plan de Movilidad Urbana Sostenible*, PMUS) of the city of Madrid, is the management tool to structure mobility policies. It allows for greater coherence in the implementation of the different municipal plans that have an impact on transport (Table 2.1). Every municipality in the Madrid region (*Comunidad Autónoma de Madrid*, CAM) has a PMUS and they follow different goals. For instance, Madrid pursues sustainability, universal accessibility, competitiveness and safety, while the municipality of Alcobendas, one of the most industrial areas in the region, aims to improve environmental conditions, reducing commuting times and improving public transport and the urban environment.

Table 2.1. Madrid municipal plans with an impact on mobility

Municipal plans	Mobility reference
General Urban Plan of Madrid	It sets the conditions for parking spaces and transport infrastructure as well as pedestrian areas and the reorganisation of space for the circulation of vehicles and people.
Local Strategy for Air Quality of the City of Madrid	It establishes measures for traffic reduction in priority areas of the city and the promotion of public transport.
Road Safety Plan	It supports one of the pillars of the mobility model: safety.
Cycling Mobility Director Plan	It includes four programmes: infrastructure, regulation, promotion and management of the network of cycling paths network.
Action Plan on Noise Pollution	To reduce noise levels, it proposes the use of quieter vehicles, the use of public transport and reduction of speed.
Plan for the Sustainable Use of Energy and Prevention of Climate Change	Its objective is to promote low-carbon mobility through sustainable transit modes such as walking, public transit, cycling and electric vehicles.

Source: Based on Municipality of Madrid (2014[20]), *Plan de movilidad Urbana Sostenible de la ciudad de Madrid*, https://www.madrid.es/UnidadesDescentralizadas/UDCMovilidadTransportes/MOVILIDAD/PMUS_Madrid_2/PMUS%20Madrid/Plan%20de%20Movilidad%20de%20Madrid%20aprobacion%20final.pdf (accessed on 17 October 2018).

Accessibility contributes to environmental strategies

Promoting accessibility is a way of contributing to environmental goals as it can reduce the need for mobility or make mobility more efficient and thus reduce emissions. According to calculations by the OECD International Transport Forum (ITF), CO_2 emissions from urban mobility will increase 26% by 2050 and demand for urban passenger transport could grow between 60%-70% in the same time, if current trends continue (ITF, 2018[21]). The increase in emissions and demand will be the result of continuous population growth, economic development and urbanisation cancelling out any CO_2 emission reductions made possible by new low and zero-carbon technologies. ITF projections indicate that total motorised mobility in cities is likely to double (+94%) between 2015 and 2050, causing a 26% increase in CO_2 emissions in urban mobility (ITF, 2018[21]). Moreover, the number of cars in cities is also expected to grow, particularly in emerging economies; in China for instance, the number of cars grew from 5.9 million in 2000 to 91.7 million in 2014. However, the number of cars per citizen in developed countries will continue to remain far above the number in emerging economies. For instance, in 2010, the United States (US) had 1 car for every 1.47 inhabitants while India had 71.4 inhabitants per car (ITF, 2018[21]).

Most of the new car owners are expected to drive in urban areas. In cities like London, UK, motorised traffic is largely responsible for the emission of pollutants into the atmosphere. Currently, road transport in London is responsible for half of the main air pollutants, with cars contributing around 14% of nitrogen oxides (NO_x) and 56% of particulate matter less than 2.5 microns in diameter ($PM_{2.5}$) emissions (Greater London Authority, 2018[13]). Figure 2.6 shows that in Greater Sydney, Australia, the combined emissions from electricity and gas used in buildings, transport and waste released 50 million tonnes of GHG into the atmosphere, equal to 54% of New South Wales' emission from these sources (Greater Sydney Commission, n.d.[22]). In New York City in the US, the transport sector accounts for 22% of the city's total greenhouse gas emissions with fossil fuels burned in passenger cars contributing 14% of the citywide total (Figure 2.7) (NYC DOT, 2016[23]).

Figure 2.6. Greater Sydney GHG emissions by sector, 2015-16

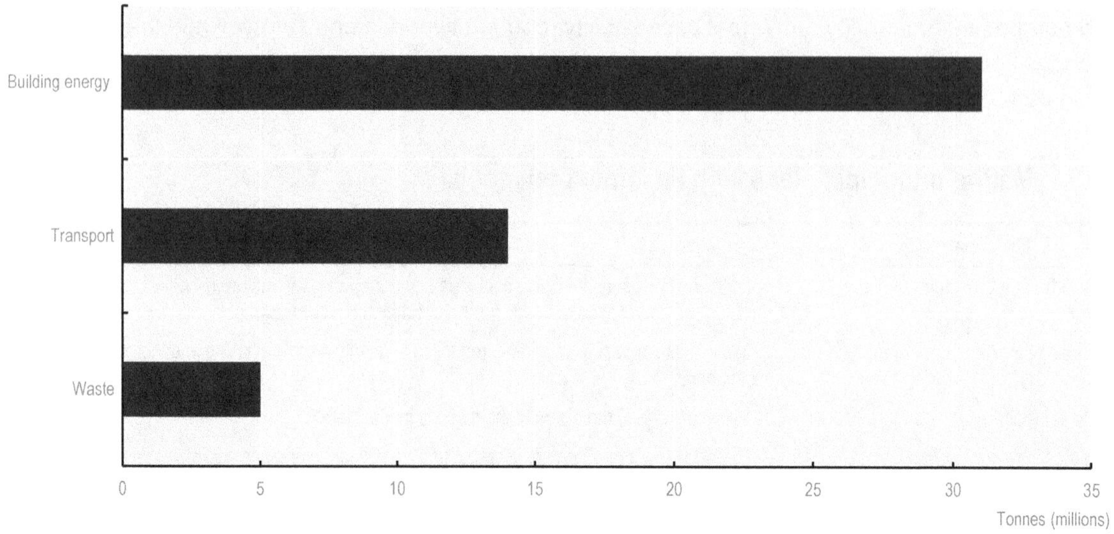

Source: Greater Sydney Commission (n.d.[22]), "Sustainability", https://www.greater.sydney/metropolis-of-three-cities/sustainability (accessed on 3 September 2019).

Figure 2.7. New York City GHG emissions by sector 2014

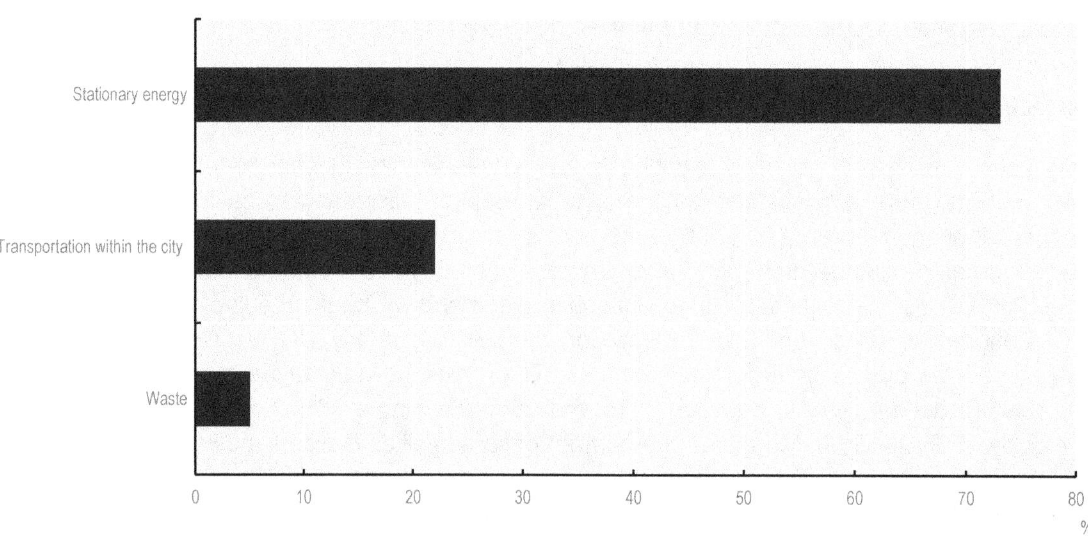

Source: NYC DOT (2016[23]), *New York City Strategic Plan 2016*, https://www.nycdotplan.nyc/PDF/Strategic-plan-2016.pdf (accessed on 6 August 2019).

Some initiatives that cities have implemented to reduce traffic congestion and emissions have been counterproductive. For instance, the region of Attica, Greece, ranks among the bottom regions in terms of air quality across the OECD. In an effort to reduce air pollution, authorities introduced a system of alternate car traffic restrictions in Athens city centre in 1982. The system allowed only cars with license plates ending with an odd number to enter a designated zone of 23 km^2 in the city centre on odd days and those with an even number on even days. The measure led to a fast rise in car ownership as many residents in Athens bought a second car with a license plate ending in a different number. The system was subsequently revised to allow less polluting vehicles to enter the zone regardless of their license plates (OECD, 2015[24]). Since 1989, Mexico City has implemented a similar system. Depending on the last digit of the plate number cars are not allowed to circulate one day a week and one Saturday a month. However, the results in air quality improvement have been very marginal. The main problem has been that authorities have focused on car restrictions and not on the substitution of cars by public transport and other less pollutant means of transport (Franco, 2017[25]). Governance co-ordination problems have also hampered any meaningful impact as the Metropolitan Zone of the Valle de Mexico (where Mexico City is located) is comprised of municipalities from three different states and there is no homogenous regulation of cars, no co-ordinated transport planning and no co-ordination in urban development (OECD, 2015[26]).

If urban mobility were based on shared and electric vehicles, CO_2 emissions from traffic could fall by 60% (ITF, 2018[21]). The problem is that the number of electric cars remains small and, to have any impact on reducing emissions, their use must be scaled up rapidly. To accelerate their adoption, governments are adopting a series of fiscal incentives taking advantage of the fact that electric vehicles are becoming more easily available and affordable. To that end, countries and cities are adopting "electro-mobility strategies" to make all public transport based on sustainable sources of power, mostly electricity. Cities in Latin America such as Bogotá, Colombia, have adopted an electro-mobility strategy to have electric, zero-emission vehicles for public transport by 2035. Moreover, Colombia's National Strategy for Electric and Sustainable Mobility aims to ensure that 10% of the vehicles bought in the country are electric by 2030. To promote the acquisition of electric vehicles, the strategy lists a number of fiscal incentives such as a 10% discount on Insurance for Traffic Accidents and a reduction in car tax to 1% of the commercial value of the vehicle.[6] In Mexico City, the bike-sharing programme is beginning to change the mobility culture and use of bikes is a growing contributor to CO_2 emissions reduction, although marginally considering the size of the city (Table 2.2).

Table 2.2. Mexico City's ECOBICI programme – Selected statistics

	2010	2011	2012	2013	2014
Journeys	841 079	2 542 963	2 737 917	6 515 328	7 952 247
Estimated CO_2 emission reduction (tonnes)	22	83	127	267	896
Estimated travel time reduction (expressed in days)	57	776	1 232	2 608	11 931

Source: OECD (2015[26]), *OECD Territorial Reviews: Valle de México, Mexico*, https://dx.doi.org/10.1787/9789264245174-en.

Another strategy to cut CO_2 emissions is to improve capacity through shared mobility. Cars operate on average 50 minutes per day with around 1.4 passengers. If car occupancy can be doubled through car sharing, today's level of mobility could be provided with less than 10% of the current number of cars, cutting CO_2 emissions by one-third without any new technology (ITF, 2018[21]). Well-planned shared mobility services can increase public transport ridership by acting as feeders.

Reducing travel demand by improving accessibility, facilitating the use of high-occupancy mobility and encouraging active mobility (walking and cycling) can help reduce CO_2 emissions from urban transport. Emissions and congestion charges on cars using urban roads have contributed to reducing local emissions by 15% and congestion by 20%-30% (ITF, 2018[21]). Thus, while improving accessibility, cities can aim to make low-carbon travel the default. In London, cycling, as a non-polluting mode of transport, is seen as part of the solution to improve air quality as it reduces emissions and noise (Transport for London, 2018[27]).

Urban planning may also contribute to CO_2 emission reduction. In Sydney, Australia, for instance, transport authorities consider that well-planned centres and cities enable a shift from private cars to public transport and active transport modes. That is why the city is working to deliver the three "30 minutes cities" (the cities that integrate Greater Sydney metropolitan area: Eastern Harbour City, Central River City and Western Parkland City). The *Greater Sydney Region Plan, A Metropolis of Three Cities* integrates land use, transport and infrastructure planning with the goal of making possible for residents to reach any destination within 30 minutes, contributing to the improvement of accessibility and sustainability (Greater Sydney Commission, n.d.[22]).

The governance of accessibility

Planning for accessibility is complex as it requires cross-cutting policies and co-ordination across policy areas and levels of government. Ensuring sustainable transport and greater accessibility across metropolitan areas and within cities requires a highly collaborative and co-ordinated process of policy and decision-making, as well as a clear division of responsibilities among actors from different policy domains. Local governments should have the administrative, legal, financial and organisational capacity to meet the goals of their strategic development plans and their transport plans or transport strategies. Infrastructure projects with deficient governance generally result in cost overruns, delays, underperformance, poor maintenance and accelerated deterioration, and expensive, underused infrastructure projects. Thus, improvements in infrastructure management and governance arrangements could lead to substantial savings and enhanced infrastructure productivity. For example, improvements in multiyear planning for infrastructure investment are essential to reinforce the governance of investment. In New Zealand, all subnational governments are required to adopt plans that layout spending and investment intentions for the coming ten years. Involving actors form the public, private and voluntary sectors in planning at different stages of public investment can lead to savings, better decisions and greater support for projects. For instance, in Germany, the decision to build a new runway at Frankfurt Airport was accompanied by a mediation process initiated by the state government of Hesse with the goal of reconciling concerns about noise and other environmental impacts with the economic case for the new runway. The process was initiated prior to the decision and included extensive consultations with proponents and opponents. A regional forum contributed to dialogue among stakeholders until the planning process was completed and the construction started (Allain-Dupré, Hulbert and Vincent, 2017[28]).

The institutional framework

Achieving accessibility requires co-operation and networks across municipalities

Promoting accessibility in metropolitan areas and regions requires the joint action of the different municipalities in the jurisdiction. Among the 668 metropolitan areas in 33 OECD countries where they have been defined, nearly 30% include 50 or more local governments in their boundaries and about 15% even contain 100 or more local governments.[7] Indeed, one feature of urbanisation is the administrative fragmentation in metropolitan areas. As cities expand, their population, built-up area and socio-economic flows spread across multiple jurisdictions. This fragmentation complicates public service delivery, in particular transport services as, in many cases, the core city is the one that carries the responsibility of providing the service for its residents and those of other municipalities. In other instances, the transport service terminates at the geographical border of the city, forcing users to make several changes to reach their final destination. To address this situation, some countries have opted for merging municipalities (e.g. Denmark) or for allowing existing municipalities to collaborate for one or more purposes, within a more or less institutionalised framework. One way of co-ordinating work across municipalities within the same jurisdiction is to establish metropolitan governance bodies. More than two-thirds of OECD metropolitan areas already have a metropolitan governance body. They are "…bodies aiming at organising responsibilities among public authorities in metropolitan areas…" (OECD, 2015, p. 17[24]). These bodies work mainly on regional development (80%), spatial planning (over 60%) and transport (over 70%) but their legal status, composition, power, budget and staff as well as their impact on policy design varies from country to country (OECD, 2015[24]).

The increase in the number of municipalities in a functional metropolitan area implies the rise in the number of municipal authorities and actors dealing with transport policy. Co-ordination among municipal authorities avoids inconsistencies in the design of routes and complexity in the ticketing system (OECD, 2015[24]). Co-operation must not only include other municipalities but also businesses and civil society, this is particularly important if it is considered that many of the cities' challenges must be faced with joint measures stretching over municipalities and competencies. For instance, for the implementation of its transport strategy, the city of Malmö has established interfaces with the regional public transport authority, the Swedish Transport Administration, the project HMSkåne for sustainable mobility and neighbouring municipalities to co-ordinate transport investments (City of Malmö, 2016[9]). In Germany, the Rhein-Main Verkehrsverbund (RMV) is the transport authority covering the metropolitan area of Frankfurt and beyond, in an area that covers approximately five million inhabitants. The RMV brings together 3 levels of government, 11 municipalities, 15 districts and the Länder of Hesse (OECD, 2015[24]). In Canada's Vancouver metropolitan area, regional transport requires co-ordinated and collaborative efforts from many stakeholders including the transport authority TransLink, Metro Vancouver[8] and the different municipalities, provincial and federal governments, the private sector, community organisations and residents. TransLink co-ordinates efforts to establish partnerships and promotes and supports reciprocal commitments to deliver policy measures, land use changes and investments needed to get the best performance out of the system. Actors form partnerships to align land use and transport planning to ensure that homes, workplaces and industrial areas are arranged in such a way that people and goods do not have to travel long distances. The partnerships work to ensure that road and transit investments are made according to the land use priorities, i.e. investments along corridors where transport connections are in place.

Transport is a policy domain that can greatly contribute to regional integration by connecting different cities and form a regional transport network, contributing to its functional integration. The Metropolitan Region of Rotterdam-The Hague (*Metropoolregio Rotterdam Den Haag*, MRDH), due to its large focus on transport, is an example of this case. Although the MRDH is not a single metropolitan area, its creation is expected to help it become one. Transport investments within the MRDH area have stimulated greater functional integration (OECD, 2016[29]). The provision of public transport is helping to bring the region closer together by not only a better provision of transport but by integrating the management and provision of public transport services into one single body for the entire region (Box 2.6).

Box 2.6. Transport as a metropolitan integration facilitator – The case of the Metropolitan Region of Rotterdam-The Hague (MRDH)

The MRDH was created in 2015 following the abolition of the eight Dutch city-regions. Rotterdam and The Hague were each at the centre of a separate city-region, which further comprised each city's surrounding municipalities. Currently, the 23 smaller neighbouring municipalities that formed the 2 city-regions form the MRDH.

The work of the MRDH is organised into two pillars: transport and economic development. The legal framework for co-operation (top-down for transport and bottom-up for economic development) is based on two parts of the same law: the Joint Regulation Act. The MRDH body created two governing committees within the MRDH joint regulation, one directing the formally transferred responsibility from the central government for public transport and one directing the voluntary inter-municipal co-operation for economic development. The largest share of the budget is dedicated to transport: EUR 480 million annually compared to approximately EUR 5.5 million for economic development. Over 96% of the transport budget is transferred from the central government. The economic development activities are funded by a EUR 2.45 contribution per inhabitant of each member municipality. The MRDH employs 85 full-time employees in its transport pillar and 15 in its economic development pillar.

One important advantage of the MRDH is its authority over a wide range of issues on mobility policy. The MRDH retained the competencies on all matters of planning and management of public transport, except railways, such as new investments, maintenance and network development. They also manage highways, traffic management, bicycle lanes, park and ride facilities and traffic safety. This permits building a more effective policy overall. Another advantage of the MRDH transport authority is that it was created before the whole area becomes highly functionally integrated. Thus, the MRDH can anticipate the mobility needs that will be generated by future metropolitan growth. Since commuting flows across the whole area are still concentrated in the two former city-regions, the MRDH has the potential to develop a mobility strategy and a transport network that can accompany more effectively the population and employment dynamics.

Source: OECD (2016[29]), *OECD Territorial Reviews: The Metropolitan Region of Rotterdam-The Hague, Netherlands*, https://dx.doi.org/10.1787/9789264249387-en.

Co-ordination across municipalities for transport planning and investment is essential to link the core city and the periphery or across suburbs. The problem is that, as the OECD points out (2015[24]), in many metropolitan areas, the transport system has not kept pace with the evolving expansion of the built-up area. It remains mostly organised in a radial structure with the main city at the core. This complicates increasing suburb-to-suburb traffic. Moreover, this situation means that most of the transport investment takes place in the core city, which is used by commuters travelling from the suburbs to work in the main city. This creates a gap between who pays for investment and those who directly benefit from using the transport network. In France, access to public transport within the cities that comprise the metropolitan area of Aix-Marseille is good; however, public transport between the urban centres of the metropolitan area is rather underdeveloped: 77% of the population living in peri-urban areas (outside the city of Marseille) has no access to public transport and only 10% of travel between Aix and Marseille is with public transport (OECD, 2015[24]). In the metropolitan area of Mexico City, for instance, the provision of transport services follows an administrative logic rather than a dynamic logic based on traffic flows (OECD, 2015[26]). In Chicago, US, approximately 36% of the population works outside the city of Chicago and 46% of workers in the city of Chicago live in the suburbs. The problem is that the division of the public transport system into an urban part (Chicago Transit Authority, CTA) and suburban part (Pace and Metra) means that CTA bus services end at the city limits where Pace services begin. Moreover, none of Metra's downtown commuter rail connects directly to the CTA rail network (OECD, 2015[24]).

Fostering accessibility requires a cross-sectoral approach and that requires inter-departmental co-operation and collaboration. A key issue is how city administrations are handling the narrow sectoral planning practices (i.e. park and landscape planners, housing planners, economic development, social services, etc). In some instances, when it comes to comprehensive planning, planners from these departments are not always invited to take part in the planning process from the start. Integrating land use, transport and environmental policies may be hindered by how responsibilities are divided not only across levels of government but also across departments within the local administration. In other cases, the number of organisations and professionals involved in substantial negotiation may compromise reaching policy decisions. A lack of a common vision may be a source of tension, which could be reflected in the different operational definitions of accessibility across the administration. For some departments, making buildings, buses and public spaces accessible for people with different physical and cognitive abilities is the priority. However, there is also a broader view that considers accessibility in terms of how people could get around in the region and have access to opportunities (goods and services), which is important for their daily lives (Gil Solá, Vilhelmson and Larsson, 2018[10]).

According to the OECD, to design and plan transport policies that increase the accessibility of urban residents to economic, social and cultural opportunities, improve multi-modality and encourage new forms of clean urban mobility, it is essential to set incentives, regulations and co-ordination mechanisms to manage trade-offs and encourage policy coherence among ministries/public agencies and across levels of government (OECD, 2019[15]).

Adopting joint working arrangements may help to produce more integrated policies for accessibility. In Copenhagen, Denmark, for example, the preparation of the transport and environment plan involved an equal number of resources and staffing from both departments. This led to a greater sense of joint ownership and collaboration between the two departments: transport and environment. Similarly, in Peterborough, UK, the transport and planning departments joined forces for the drafting of the city centre master plan. There was equal involvement in the process and equal interest in finding policies to fulfil planning and transport goals (Stead and Geerlings, 2005[30]).

The role of a metropolitan transport authority

One agency in the institutional framework that facilitates implementation of the transport strategy is a metropolitan-wide transport authority. The creation of transport authorities responsible for the organisation and provision of transport services in multiple jurisdictions in a metropolitan area is increasingly common. The creation of this kind of body requires clear buy-in from all levels of government as well as private operators (OECD, 2015[24]). According to World Bank research, the key essential elements for ensuring the sustainability and suitability of a lead transport institution are:

- *Public value*: it must contribute to advance societal good.
- *Internal capacity*: it must have the technical and financial capacities to perform its tasks.
- *External and political support*: it should have support from the highest political levels to ensure resources are made available to build organisational capacity (Kumar and Agarwal, 2013[31]).

Another feature that supports the proper operation of metropolitan transport authorities is a clear definition of responsibilities to avoid overlap with other institutions. For example, in Metro Vancouver, the metropolitan transport authority has responsibility for regional transit and commuting options and shares with the municipalities the responsibility for the major road network and regional cycling. Examples of bodies with similar responsibilities are: Transport for London (TfL), the *Consorcio Regional de Transportes de Madrid* (CRTM), the South Coast British Columbia Transport Authority (TransLink), the Regional Organiser of Prague Integrated Transport (ROPID) and the *Île de France Mobilités*. These organisations usually bring together all local governments located in the metropolitan area. These authorities manage a wide range of transport such as metro, bus, trams, suburban trains, ferries and others. It is worth noting that some transport authorities also have responsibility for the maintenance of infrastructures such as pavements, bridges, tunnels, streets and motorways. In other cases, they manage taxes or charges directly. The mere existence of a transport authority, however, does not in itself guarantee better policy co-ordination. The reason is that metropolitan areas continue to evolve, even once well-functioning governance structures may eventually need to be adapted. For example, in the Prague metropolitan area, the transport authority ROPID does not cover the entire metropolitan area, more and more inhabitants from other municipalities in the Bohemia Region commute to Prague for work and the lack of transport options leads to an increase in the use of private cars.

There is no common blueprint that defines the responsibilities of a transport authority (Box 2.7). Some transport authorities are direct providers of transport services (e.g. TfL and TransLink), while others co-ordinate the work of different service providers (CRTM, *Île-de-France Mobilités*, ROPID and RMV). However, some typical responsibilities of transport authorities emerge:

- Planning the transport system by ensuring the provision of the services across the metropolitan area and discouraging the use of private vehicles.
- Managing the operation or co-ordinating the operation of transport services.
- Defining investment projects on mobile and fix infrastructure.
- Co-ordinating the planning of transport service provision across municipalities in the metropolitan area.
- Ensuring intermodality to facilitate the movement of people and goods and make the most of the existing infrastructure.

- Setting fees and tariffs for transport services across the metropolitan area.
- Planning and managing the network of roads and traffic lights.
- Contributing to the achievement of regional development objectives (i.e. housing, environmental, economic) through transport provision.

Box 2.7. Examples of public transport authorities

- **Île-de-France Mobilités** (ex-STIF) is the transport authority for the Île-de-France region. It is in charge of organising and financing the existing transport network in the region as well as the renovation of the rolling stock. It co-ordinates a network of metro, trams, trains–RER and buses. It is jointly supervised by the region of Île-de-France, the departments that make up the region and the city of Paris. It manages a budget of EUR 10 billion for the functioning of the transport in the entire region. The agency assumes a broad range of public transport planning responsibilities that include defining general operational and service-level targets, setting fares and negotiating performance-based contracts with public service providers such as the *Régie autonome des transports parisiens* (RATP). *Île-de-France Mobilités* also develops an Urban Mobility Plan (*Plan de déplacements urbains*, PDU) that includes land use and transport plans to guide all lower levels of government. The programme of actions included in the PDU is subject to approval from regional, general and municipal councils, transport users, experts and environmental associations. Revenue from a dedicated transport tax (*versement transport*) levied on employers and based on payrolls has enabled the agency to extend and maintain the public transport network and non-motorised transport facilities.
- **Transport for London** (TfL) is an integrated body responsible for London's transport system. Its role is to implement the Mayor's Transport Strategy and manage the provision of transport services in the capital city. TfL manages buses, the London Underground, the Docklands Light Railway, the London Overground and London Trams. It is also responsible for managing the London River Services, running Victoria Coach Station and the congestion charge scheme. The body also has responsibility for a network of main roads, all of London's 6 000 traffic lights and regulates taxis and private car share.
- **South Coast British Columbia Transport Authority** (TransLink) is a statutory authority responsible for the regional transportation network of Metro Vancouver, British Columbia, Canada. TransLink's purpose is to move people and goods. It is responsible for planning, managing and operating the regional transportation system that supports Metro Vancouver's Regional Growth Strategy, air quality and GHG reduction objectives and the economic development of the region. It manages the bus system throughout the region, the Sky Train rapid transit, SeaBus passenger ferries, West Coast Express commuter rail, and HandyDART for passengers who are unable to use conventional transit. Its vision is to make Metro Vancouver a better place to live by building on transportation excellence. The mission is to connect the region and enhance its liveability by providing a sustainable transportation network, embraced by communities and people.
- **Regional Organiser of Prague Integrated Transport** (*Regionální organizátor Pražké integrované dopravy*, ROPID) is the municipal contributory organisation owned by the city of Prague responsible for the operation of the Prague Integrated Transport. Its basic tasks include organising and designing transport, co-ordinating the operations of multiple providers, setting quality standards, discussing traffic solutions and their funding with subsidy providers and transport operators, negotiating contracts and supervising operators' performance, organising financial flows of revenues and subsidies within the PID system, setting tariffs and fares within the PID system and checking and marketing the system. It co-ordinates the activities of

22 operators that provide public transport service in the Prague metropolitan area. The biggest transport operator is the Prague Public Transit Company (DPP), owned by the city of Prague, which operates the metro, trams and most bus lines. ROPID also conducts transport quality monitoring (punctuality, cleanliness, information), passenger counting (on stops and in vehicles), and conducts passenger surveys (travel behaviour).

- **Consorcio Regional de Transportes de Madrid** (CRTM) is the public transport authority of the Madrid region (CAM). It is an autonomous and technical agency in charge of co-ordinating public transport policies across municipalities and different providers. It assumes the integrated management of collective public transport in the CAM (metro, light rail, public bus operators, private bus operators) but not for individual transport modes such as taxis, school transport or shared-bicycles; competency for these transport modes reside in the city councils. The CRTM is in charge of: i) planning public transport infrastructure; ii) establishing an integrated fare system for the whole public transport network; iii) developing a management policy and a stable and clear finance framework for the public transport system; iv) planning services and defining the co-ordinated operational programmes for all transport modes; v) auditing the integration of public transport with new urban planning; among others.
- **Department of Transportation New York City** (DOT) is in charge of providing safe, efficient and environmentally responsible movement of people and goods and maintains and enhances the transportation infrastructure including bridges, tunnels, streets, sidewalks and highways. DOT manages an annual operating budget of USD 900 million and a 5-year USD 10.1 billion capital programme.
- **Rhein-Main Transport Association** (RMV) is the single authority over public transport in the metropolitan area of Frankfurt. It brings together 3 levels of government; 11 municipalities, 15 districts and the Länder of Hesse. It defines metropolitan transport policy and is in charge of planning, investment decisions, price setting and co-ordinating 153 public and private operators (subway, bus, suburban railway and trains). It integrates regional and local transport under uniform and needs-based rules for the entire metropolitan area: one timetable, one price, one ticket. RMV covers its costs at 57% with the remainder coming from federal regionalisation funds passed through the state budget and form municipalities via state financial equalisation.

Source: For Île-de-France Mobilités: Île-de-France Mobilités (n.d.[32]), *Le réseau*, https://www.iledefrance-mobilites.fr/le-reseau/; For TfL: ORR (n.d.[33]), *Who We Work With – Governments*, https://orr.gov.uk/about-orr/who-we-work-with/government/transport-for-london; For TransLink: Metro Vancouver Regional District (2011[34]), *Regional Growth Strategy - Metro Vancouver 2040: Shaping Our Future*, http://www.metrovancouver.org/services/regional-planning/PlanningPublications/RGSAdoptedbyGVRDBoard.pdf (accessed on 5 April 2018), TransLink (2013[35]), *Regional Transportation Strategy: Strategic Framework*, https://www.translink.ca/-/media/Documents/plans_and_projects/regional_transportation_strategy/rts_strategic_framework_07_31_2013.pdf (accessed on 29 March 2018) and TransLink (n.d.[36]), *Learn More About Us*, https://www.translink.ca/About-Us.aspx; For ROPID: ROPID (2018[37]), *Prague Integrated Transport and ROPID*, ROPID, Prague and ROPID (n.d.[38]), *We Introduce ROPID*, http://stary.ropid.cz/info/we-introduce-ropid__s219x902.html; For CRTM: García Pastor, A. (2015[39]), "Integration of the public transport system in Madrid region", https://www.slideshare.net/EMBARQNetwork/integration-of-the-public-transport-system-in-madrid-region (accessed on 1 October 2018) and CRTM (n.d.[40]), *Conócenos*, https://www.crtm.es/conocenos.aspx; For DOT: DOT (n.d.[41]), *About*, https://www1.nyc.gov/html/dot/html/about/about.shtml; For RMV: OECD (2015[24]), *Governing the City*, https://doi.org/10.1787/9789264226500-en (accessed on 9 August 2017).

Transport authorities co-ordinate their planning work with that of bodies in charge of spatial planning to ensure coherent metropolitan plans. In metropolitan Vancouver, for instance, TransLink and the Metro Vancouver Regional District (planning authority) co-ordinate their work to ensure coherence in the definition and implementation of the Regional Growth Strategy. In Chicago, two different agencies are responsible for transport and spatial planning. The Chicago Metropolitan Agency for Planning (CMAP) develops a comprehensive regional plan integrating transport and land use for seven counties, whereas the Regional Transportation Authority (RTA) co-ordinates the three public transport service boards (Chicago Transit Authority [CTA], Metra and Pace) (OECD, 2015[24]). However, co-ordinating transport and spatial planning at the regional level is not always the norm. In Madrid, Spain, the lack of a regional development strategy hinders that co-ordination. The transport authority has to co-ordinate with each one of the municipalities of the region to ensure investments correspond to local needs.

In many cities, such as Frankfurt, London, Madrid, Paris and Prague, the transport authority helped introduce a harmonised fare structure. A harmonised fare structure is a basic element in ensuring easy and affordable use of public transport. Nevertheless, other metropolitan areas still operate fragmented fare systems. For example, in Marseille, France, ten public transport authorities operating in the larger metropolitan area, including six transport organising authorities (*autorités organisatrices des transports*, AOT) that cover each of the six existing municipal authorities. Despite progress in terms of sharing information on investment plans and pricing systems, public transport fares are yet to be harmonised (OECD, 2015[24]). Korea introduced a fare collection system at a quasi-national scale through the single mobility and smart payment card throughout the country called T-money. This system allows users to ride most public transport systems in the country with a single pass and benefit from discounts when they transfer from one mode to another, encouraging public transport use and multi-modality (OECD, 2017[42]).

Box 2.8. Korea's single mobility pass

In 2004, the city of Seoul launched a revolutionary fare payment method called the T-money card. The Korea Smart Card Corporation (KSCC) (owned 34.4% by the city of Seoul, 31.85% by LG CNS and 15.73% by Credit Card Union) developed and operated the system. The T-money card can be used on buses and/or subways in different metropolitan cities and locations across Korea, including Busan, Daegu, Daejeon, Gyeonggi, Gwangju, Incheon, Sejong, Seoul and other provinces. There are now 11 transport card companies (including KSCC) operating in different cities and provinces through direct service contracts with subnational authorities. Beyond these conventional pre-paid services, ten commercial banks nationwide also topped their own credit or debit cards with a public transport card function, with deferred payment.

By using this pass (either a card, phone or T-money enabled device), travellers can obtain discounts and save themselves avoid having to purchase single-journey tickets for every ride. Discounts can be effective on rides with transfers from one bus to another, one subway line to another, or from bus to subway or vice versa. Transfer discounts are applicable for up to 4 times a day, within a transfer time limit of 30 minutes (up to 1 hour from 9pm to 7am the next day). The user simply needs to tap his device on the sensors as he/she gets off the bus or exits the subway. Many taxis also accept payment via T-money.

In 2014, the Ministry of Land, Infrastructure and Transport expanded the service to integrate the public transport fare collection system throughout most of the country. The new pass is accepted in all buses, subways, taxis, trains, intercity buses, express buses, tollgates and even major retailers. The pass costs about KRW 3 500 (approximately USD 3) and can be purchased and recharged at subway stations, bank ATMs, convenience stores and kiosks located adjacent to bus stops. This enables seamless journeys both in terms of intermodal and inter-regional transport, allowing for new levels of user convenience that are rarely achieved in other countries.

Source: OECD (2017[42]), *Urban Transport Governance and Inclusive Development in Korea*, https://dx.doi.org/10.1787/9789264272637-en.

Accessibility requires co-ordination across levels of government to reduce transaction costs

The success of any transport and accessibility strategy also depends on how intergovernmental relations are structured. The reason is that local authorities are not always the financier of transport infrastructure or services as other actors are normally involved such as national or regional authorities as well as private sector companies or individual concessionaries. Co-operation and co-ordination are two key elements of these relations as they facilitate the exchange of information, planning, effective and efficient use of financial resources, and avoidance of duplication of programmes and projects. In the UK for instance, local transport plans have a 5-year time horizon, while regional spatial strategies have a spatial vision for a 20-year time horizon and the national government has a 10-year transport investment plan. This therefore requires co-ordination, negotiation and sometimes trade-offs.

The allocation of responsibilities across levels of government requires coherent multi-modal, multiyear strategic planning that is not always easy to implement in metropolitan areas (OECD, 2015[24]). Setting up a clear division of responsibilities for expenditure across levels of government could go a long way in improving co-ordination and reducing transaction costs in service delivery such as transport and the construction of infrastructure. Generally, national or central government is involved in overall policy, setting standards and auditing; state/regional governments have an oversight function; and local governments are in charge of the provision of infrastructure and services. However, designing a clear-cut allocation of competencies across levels of government is a highly complex process. The interdependency of many services and policy areas require the intervention of all levels of government. In addition, the assignment of government responsibilities is not always appropriate, either because of overlaps in responsibilities or because some policy domains are not specifically assigned to any level of government and require co-operation.

In Korea, for example, building the different types of roads that integrate the road network requires the participation of different levels of government and specialised institutions. The Ministry of Land, Infrastructure and Transport (MOLIT) is the main authority in charge but it may delegate responsibilities to the Korea Expressway Corporation (for the construction, maintenance and management of national expressways), while subnational governments are responsible for provincial, metropolitan and local roads as well as national highways that go through the cities (Table 2.3 and OECD (2016[43])).

Other areas such as road safety may require the intervention of an even wider set of actors. MOLIT co-ordinated the road safety planning framework by collecting inputs from other ministries and subnational levels of government to prepare the Five-year Transportation Safety Master Plan that covers all modes of transport. The master plan should be reflected in the Provincial and Local Transportation Safety Master Plans, prepared every five years and implemented through yearly action plans. However, the responsibility for road safety is still highly fragmented as there are other actors engaged in one or more activities. For example, in broad terms: engineering is addressed by MOLIT, supported by its affiliated organisation, the Korea Transportation Safety Authority (KoTSA); enforcement by the National Police Agency, supported by its affiliated organisation, the KoROAD; and education by the Ministry of Education. Each of these axes also involves other stakeholders from different ministries and agencies, other levels of government and civil society organisations (OECD, 2016[43]).

Table 2.3. Governance of road infrastructure in Korea

Authorities in charge of the different types of roads in Korea

Type of road	Authority in charge	Design	Budget allocated for:		
			Construction	Land use	Maintenance and management
National expressways	MOLIT	National	National 50% Korea Expressway 50%	National	Korea Expressway Corporation
National highways					
Outside cities	MOLIT		National	National	National
Inside cities	Mayors		Local	Local	Local
National bypass	MOLIT		National	National	National
Provincial roads					
Provincial roads supported by the national government	Governor (TL3 region) or mayor (if inside a city)	National (executed by local)	National (executed by local)	Local	Local
Provincial roads	Governor (TL3 region) or mayor (if inside a city)		Local	Local	Local
Metropolitan roads or city/gun/gu roads	Mayor or head of gun		Local	Local	Local

Source: OECD (2016[43]), *Road Infrastructure, Inclusive Development and Traffic Safety in Korea*, https://dx.doi.org/10.1787/9789264255517-en.

Financing accessibility

Cities need to explore other potential sources of funding for transport

For cities to deliver their transport strategies and promote accessibility that improves quality of life, health and social integration, it is essential to explore additional sources of income. Appropriate additional income sources depend on the specific context of each country or city and their political-administrative system. Diversification to external sources of financing is needed to invest in infrastructure. OECD studies show that such diversification, through private funding, public-private partnerships (PPPs) or funding through financial markets via inter-municipal borrowing remains very limited at the subnational levels of government (Allain-Dupré, Hulbert and Vincent, 2017[28]). Part of the reason is the complexity of using PPPs and the extensive legal and technical capacities required, which most subnational governments do not possess. However, devolution or decentralisation processes, the adoption of land value capture mechanisms, the creation of partnerships and the participation of the private sector in transport are four areas that could be explored.

Box 2.9. How subnational governments are funded

Generally, subnational governments are funded by five main sources of revenues: tax revenue, grants and subsidies, user charges and fees, property income and other revenues. The level of each of these items depends on the level of fiscal autonomy every city has and on the political organisation of a country (federation vs. unitary states). Subnational governments in Romania, for instance, are still dependent on central government transfers, which constitute the bulk of their revenue (81.9%), while tax revenues are still limited (10.8%).[9]

According to the World Observatory on Subnational Government Finance and Investment, grants and subsidies are the primary source of revenue in the great majority of countries around the world. There are, however, great variations across countries in terms of share of GDP and share of total subnational revenue. Taxes account for 32.7% of subnational revenue and 3.3% of GDP. Moreover, subnational government tax revenues account for 14.9% of public tax revenue.

According to the OECD Principles on Urban Policy, there are several ways by which countries and cities could harness adequate funding for the implementation of urban projects, infrastructure and services, such as:

- Promoting a diversified, balanced and sustainable basket of resources.
- Using economic instruments such as taxes or fees to catalyse revenues.
- Providing subnational governments with sufficient leeway to adjust and manage their revenue.
- Mobilising innovative financing tools: borrowing, land value capture mechanisms and infrastructure funds.
- Leveraging private sector funding when appropriate.

Source: OECD/UCLG (2019[44]), "2019 Report World Observatory on Subnational Government Finance and Investment: Key findings", http://www.sng-wofi.org/publications/2019_SNG-WOFI_REPORT_Key_Findings.pdf (accessed on 28 August 2019); OECD (2019[15]), *OECD Principles on Urban Policy*, http://www.oecd.org/cfe/ (accessed on 16 March 2020).

Devolution or decentralisation

Local governments generally control relatively little of the tax raised within their boundaries. Funding is therefore heavily reliant on national government grants. Devolving or granting more financial powers to cities could allow them to manage their own growth. Moreover, granting cities more revenue-raising powers can promote accountability, fairness and economic efficiency. For example, it has been suggested that to increase tax autonomy for local governments in the US would be to increase their reliance on local income taxes rather than on property tax and for states to reduce or eliminate some of the restrictions currently imposed on local property taxes (Reschovsky, 2019[45]). In London, the Mayor's Transport Strategy promotes devolving more financial powers to London and other UK cities to allow them more control over their own growth. It proposes to seek additional taxes, financial powers or other similar mechanisms such as Vehicle Excise Duty in London to create a fairer way of funding the delivery of transport schemes and better capture and conserve the benefits they create (Greater London Authority, 2018[13]). The fiscal dimension of decentralisation is very often the weakest or missing link. One of the most common challenges is the misalignment between responsibilities allocated to subnational governments and the resources available to them (OECD, 2019[46]).

Land value capture mechanisms

Land value capture is considered a strong financial tool for transport funding (Medda, 2012[47]; OECD, 2015[26]). The basic premise is that by establishing a close relationship between land development planning and transport accessibility, cities can create and increase economic, social and environmental urban value. It allows public transport authorities to extract part of the land value benefits that public transport (or other infrastructure investments) provide in order to fund further developments. There are at least two channels for capturing the land value uplift. The first one is through the selling or leasing of development rights around the transit assets; the other is through taxation-based schemes that target users, nearby landowners and other beneficiaries (Olajide and Arcé, 2017[48]). Betterment tax, accessibility increment contribution (AIC) and joint development are three land value capture mechanisms that can be implemented in combination according to the urban context (Medda, 2012[47]). Based on residents' willingness to pay for accessibility and a less congested and polluted city, policymakers can then correctly allocate the incentive for the transport investment and, at the same time, define an equitable and transparent land value capture mechanism (Medda, 2012[47]).

Table 2.4. Examples of land value capture (LVC) mechanisms in practice

LVC mechanism	Definition	Examples
Betterment tax	This is a tax on the land value-added by public investment and is directed towards the beneficiaries of increased accessibility, of reduced congestion and pollution, and of lower transport costs.	Both Hong Kong (China) and Singapore have financed their transport infrastructure and services (i.e. metro systems) through LVC. The betterment taxes in Hong Kong are based on full market value and in Singapore the tax is about 50% of full market value. The Singapore government decided to leave some of the windfall benefits to the private sector to incentivise urban development. It leases, with different restrictions, the land around stations to the MRT Corporation.
Accessibility increment contribution (AIC)	This refers to the fiscal incentive instruments that earmark future revenues (fiscal contribution for accessibility increment) to finance current expenditure. The basic idea is that public improvement expenditures induce growth in urban areas characterised for low accessibility.	Private sector development of specific hubs of the public transport network can be conducted through AIC. Large stations with high levels of footfall represent a clear opportunity for commercial and business property development. In Brazil, Belo Horizonte and Porto Allegre transfer stations of their respective Bus Rapid Transit (BRT) systems have been developed under AIC.
Joint development (financialisation)	In a joint development project, to finance and maximise the profitability of transport investment and the increase of accessibility, the local government encourages property development (residential and/or commercial) close to stations. It includes air rights development, ground-lease arrangements, connection-fee programmes and other incentives to promote real estate development.	In the US, several joint development projects are found within transit-oriented development (TOD), pedestrian-friendly and public transport supportive development or redevelopment where private sector intervention has represented a feasible solution for new financial resources. In Denmark, TOD, a fully integrated transport planning approach, has been used for the development of the new town Ørestad. The new transport system and improved accessibility have been financed on the basis of commercial rate borrowing.

Source: Elaborated based on Medda, F. (2012[47]), "Land value capture finance for transport accessibility: A review", http://dx.doi.org/10.1016/j.jtrangeo.2012.07.013.

Creation of public partnerships for funding transport investment

The experience of Metro Vancouver suggests that finding the right mix of funding sources in the short and long terms requires the creation of partnerships between the federal, provincial and local government level. In Metro Vancouver, partnerships are created to fund major capital initiatives that connect the region, support the economy and create sustainable communities. These types of projects are considered generational as they produce local, regional, provincial and national benefits in the longer term. Their funding is ensured by all levels of government. Since local communities also benefit from major capital investments as they generate higher land values, bring incremental tax revenue and support city-building objectives, they are responsible for ensuring that formal partnerships are in place. The Mayors' Council,[10] TransLink and host municipalities develop partnership agreements for ten-year investments plans. Any municipal financial contribution is intended to cost-share for a specific project providing both regional and local impact. Contributions may be one-time, ongoing or property contributions towards direct construction costs. Local financial contributions may take the form of in-kind contributions (Mayors' Council on Regional Transportation, 2017[18]). TransLink contributions to project investments are defined in the agreements and may include: project investment commitments (capital, operating and phasing), planning and process commitments, transportation service and system integration, and funding, etc.

Private sector participation in urban transport financing

The public sector can fund public transport infrastructure by providing the resources from general funds or taxation. In this case, the capital is not expected to be recovered. Transport infrastructure can also be financed by the private sector and, in this case, the capital is expected to be recovered (Rodrigue, 2020[49]). Given the extent of investment needs and the constraints in public finances, cities need to mobilise private investment. Governments have a key role in mobilising private investment in transport infrastructure by establishing reform agendas that deliver "investment-grade policies". Chile, for instance, has been successful in mobilising private finance in the development of its infrastructure. The country adopted and refined the concessions model for delivering infrastructure, a major factor that facilitated building its extensive motorway network. Since 1992, Chile has procured 82 projects worth USD 19 billion and built and rehabilitated 2 500 km of motorways using the concession mechanism (OECD, 2017[50]). "An integrated framework with clear and stable climate and transport policies, sound investment policies, and targeted and innovative tools is essential to overcome barriers to private sector investments in sustainable transport" (OECD, n.d., p. 6[51]). The OECD Green Investment Policy Framework provides a non-prescriptive list of policies, tools and instruments available to policymakers to scale up private investment toward sustainable transport infrastructure.

Table 2.5. OECD Green Investment Policy Framework

Action	Elements/tools
1. Strategic goal setting and policy alignment	• Adopting long-term targets and clear policy goals, and integrating sustainable transport goals within infrastructure plans. • Adopting a co-benefits approach. • Mainstreaming the use of multi-criteria cost-benefit analyses to assess the full environmental, social and economic costs and benefits of transport infrastructure. • Integrating land use and transport planning.
2. Enabling policies and incentives	• Promote sound investment principles and open and competitive access to sustainable transport infrastructure. • Adopt adequate pricing mechanism to address market and government failures (carbons prices, fuel and vehicle taxes, reform of fossil fuel subsidies, congestion charges, parking levies). • Complement carbon pricing schemes with supply-side regulations and policies (i.e. zoning policies and land use planning); public procurement programmes; and standard-setting (i.e. building codes and design standards).

Action	Elements/tools
3. Transitional financial policies and instruments	• PPPs allow risk-sharing but they must offer sufficient value for money compared to traditional public procurement. • Land value capture tools to obtain revenues from the indirect and proximity benefits generated by transport infrastructure such as an increase in real estate value to help fund transport projects. • Loans, grants and loan guarantees are traditional financial tools used to leverage private investment in large-scale infrastructure projects. • Green bonds which have the potential to attract institutional investors such as pension funds and insurance companies, by tapping into the debt capital markets currently underexploited for sustainable transport investment. • Short-run subsidies to provide transitional support to sustainable transport options and technologies.
4. Harness resources and build capacity	• Effective transport planning may ensure proper project implementation, foster innovation and harness resources in support of sustainable transport goals. • Investor capacity gaps may need to be addressed which may be due to lack of data or expertise. • Climate risk assessment is needed to mainstream climate resilience in transport planning.
5. Promote green business and consumer behaviour	• Information, education, public awareness campaigns and business outreach programmes can help reduce information barriers, promote changes in corporate and consumer behaviour, encouraging the use of transport. • Individuals and private actors need reliable information on which to base their travel and investment decisions.

Source: Adapted from OECD (n.d.[51]), *Mobilising Private Investment in Sustainable Transport Infrastructure*, https://www.oecd.org/env/cc/financing-transport-brochure.pdf (accessed on 27 August 2019).

Cities need to consider adopting a medium-term budget framework for transport investment

A medium-term budget framework[11] may help cities promote more efficient use of resources by creating stable and predictable conditions to plans their investment expenditures. A medium-term budget framework has the potential to facilitate multiyear planning, spend resources as needed and identify and exploit efficiency-related savings. Official spending authorisations would still remain annual but a medium-term budget framework can enable transport authorities, as well as any other government ministry or agency, to make clearer commitments in their budget allocations. Transport authorities would be in a better position to plan their investment projects and activities. According to the International Monetary Fund (IMF), the efficiency of infrastructure investment can be increased by providing budget actors with more time to design projects, negotiate contracts, identify risks and manage synergies (Harris et al., 2013[52]). A multiyear planning horizon would allow governments to relax some of the limits or constraints on transport agencies, limits or constraints that can otherwise encourage inefficient use of resources.

Sources of revenue for transport funding are limited and costs are increasing

Cities are more frequently experiencing problems to finance transport investment. Some cities and regional governments have adopted efficiency programmes to reduce operating costs. However, the costs of commuting are still growing. In New South Wales (Australia), the level of taxpayer funding for transport has increased on average 4.5% per annum since 2012 and it is expected to reach AUD 5.7 billion per year by 2026 (AUD 2 billion above 2018's level) (NSW Government, 2018[12]).[12]

Transport investment is generally funded through a combination of fares, dedicated taxes and subsidies by municipal or higher levels of government. The lack of reliable and adequate sources of funding is undermining cities' capacities to plan for long-term transport investment projects. Nowadays, public transport infrastructure financing faces several challenges such as: i) the lack of sufficient funding for maintaining and improving the transport network; ii) divergence of purpose as transport initiatives should be designed to promote productivity gains (accessibility, capacity and performance) but many projects are politically driven; and iii) the misalignment between the time horizon of the infrastructure project (normally long-term) and the time horizon of the financing (normally short-term) (Rodrigue, 2020[49]).

Governments also tend to use PPPs to finance investment in transport and infrastructure. Research suggests that private investment may lead to efficiency gains and increased consumer welfare if appropriate organisational, institutional and regulatory conditions are met (Makovšek, 2019[53]). Most private investment flows into road infrastructure projects where there is no evidence of improved value for money. PPPs in sectors with little to no competition like road and rail services may have difficulty in ensuring value for money due to failures in risk pricing that are typical in the PPP model. The ITF has found that private investment cannot close the infrastructure gap as a PPP is a financing vehicle (to borrow money) and an investment gap is a funding problem. A financing solution cannot resolve a funding problem. Thus, if the government cannot afford to finance a project through the use of public funds, it will not be able to afford it as a PPP (Makovšek, 2019[53]). To improve the potential of PPPs in financing investments in transport, the ITF recommends four lines of action:

- Pursue private infrastructure investment on the basis of efficiency.
- Collect and analyse the data necessary to determine when PPPs lead to greater efficiency.
- Upgrade accounting standards to offset any bias in favour of PPPs.
- Learn how to improve PPPs in general and when to replace them with alternative models (Makovšek, 2019[53]).

The lack of proper funding and the financial vulnerability of strategic organisations working in the transport sector prevent investment in maintenance and expansion of the transport network. In Romania, for instance, limited financial resources and poor management have prevented the modernisation of the country's rail infrastructure. Moreover, Romania's state-owned enterprises (SOEs) play a key role in the transport sector and are responsible for building and maintaining rail and road infrastructure and delivering services. However, SOEs are large, inefficient and financially vulnerable according to the IMF (2015[54]). Efficiency and profitability of many SOEs have been weak and have been unable to generate resources for urgently needed investment. In the Chicago Tri-State Metro-Region in the US, the Regional Transportation Authority (RTA), which serves 6 counties and 88% of the population in the metropolitan region, dedicates most of its funding to operations (USD 2 billion annually) rather than on maintenance or capital investment as operating costs have increased 4.5% annually. Moreover, half of RTA's operating costs are financed by fares and other system-related revenues such as advertising and concessions, with the remainder supplied by an RTA sales tax applied based on proximity to Chicago and Cook County, a real estate transfer tax in the city of Chicago, and state matching funds and contributions. Capital funds come from federal and state sources (OECD, 2012[55]). In Metro Vancouver, TransLink has taxation authority (fuel tax portion, levies, project toll charges, property tax, motor vehicle charges and small fees) and one-third of its revenues come from transit fares (Government of British Columbia, 1998[56]), which are used to fund transport investment plans. The Canadian federal government contributes 40% of the funding. Funding the 10-Year Transport Vision requires CAD 7 billion[13] to cover major infrastructure investment and increases in bus services.

Financing public transport is a balancing game between citizens' desire for low fares and costs of operation and investment. Figure 2.8 shows a positive correlation between public transport fares and per capita GDP in cities around the OECD. In many cases, cities offer low fares, discounts and exemptions to make it affordable to specific population groups (e.g. the elderly, students, the unemployed). This means that city administrations have to dedicate large sums of public money in public transport subsidies. High subsidies result in less available funds for maintenance, inspections, infrastructure upgrading and replacement of rolling stock. For instance, the city of Kyiv, Ukraine, has spent about 6% of its total budget on operating subsidies over the last 5 years (OECD, 2018[57]).

The transfers that cities receive from national governments may also vary depending on the level of the economic strength of every city, which determines the availability of resources for transport investment. In

Madrid, funding for public transport in the metropolitan region comes from a combination of contributions and subsidies that are co-ordinated through an investment programme managed by the metropolitan transport authority (*Consorcio Regional de Transportes de Madrid*, CRTM). The financial needs of the transport system consist on a compensation per service supplied paid by the CRTM to the different operators and it is funded by public contributions from all levels of government (central, regional and municipal) and from users. In France, the cost of transport in Île-de-France is about EUR 10 billion per year, of which 28% comes from tickets and travel cards sales and 72% is financed by employers, local governments and other revenues.[14] In Chile's capital Santiago, the operating costs of the mobility network *Transantiago* increased by 64% between 2009 and 2018 and fares by 70% over the same period. In 2019, the *Transantiago* system was changed to *Red Metropolitana de Movilidad* (RED) which is 50% financed by fares and 50% by the state.[15] In Warsaw, Poland, funding particular transport infrastructure projects require a mixture of local, national and European funds. It uses city budgets, bank loans – including loans from the European Investment Bank (EIB) – and EU funds (mainly the Cohesion Fund). Romania's modernisation of its railway network depends on EU funds (Box 2.10). Malmö's Sustainable Urban Mobility Plan in Sweden also foresees that for the implementation of some of its actions and processes, external funding can be applied for from the state, the region and the EU (City of Malmö, 2016[9]).

Figure 2.8. Comparison of public transport fares and city GDP per capita

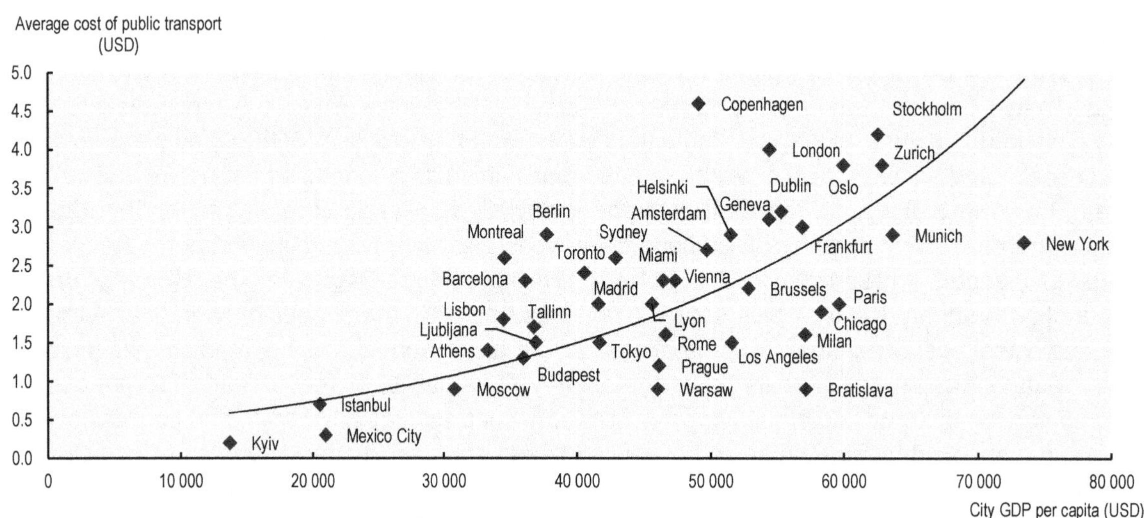

Source: OECD (2018[57]), *Maintaining the Momentum of Decentralisation in Ukraine*, https://dx.doi.org/10.1787/9789264301436-en.

Box 2.10. Financing public transport projects via external sources: Warsaw and Romania

Warsaw metro line 2

In 2015, the city of Warsaw, Poland, announced plans to extend line 2 of the city's metro system. In 2017, the EU approved the allocation of EUR 432 million through the Cohesion Fund. The extension will connect the city's east and west areas. The European resources will cover the construction of the six new metro stations: three on the line's northeast segment (Trocka, Targówek and Szwedzka) and three on the western section (Księcia Janusza, Młynów and Płocka). The funds will also cover the construction of a technical terminal and the procurement of 13 trains and the preparation works of the project.

In 2016, the EIB announced financing for EUR 896 million out of the EUR 1.8 billion necessary for metro line 2. The general project includes the construction of 16.4 km of line and 14 stations, the building of a depot and the procurement of 59 trains of which 22 will replace the existing rolling stock on line 1 and the remaining 37 will be in service on line 2. With the 6.5 km extension, line 2 will measure 13.5 km and works are expected to be completed at the end of 2019.

Romania railway network

Romania uses EU funds for financing train programmes (85%) and only a minimal part comes from the state budget (15%). Between 2007 and 2013, EU funding -European Regional Development Fund (ERDF) + Cohesion Fund + Trans-European Transport Network (TEN-T)- of Romania's railway reached EUR 1.9 billion. This financing was fully allocated to sections of a major rail route: the north branch (Constanta-Braşov-Curtici) of the former TEN-T Priority Project 22. Recently, EU funds, through the TENT-T initiative, have been used to rehabilitate 89.5 km of double-track railway line that connects communities in the central and western regions connecting the municipalities of Sighişoara and Coşlariu in the Transylvania region. This section of the railway is part of a line that connects the city of Braşov located in the central region to the Hungarian border crossing the western region. The total investment for the project "Rehabilitation of the Railway Line Braşov – Simeria at Section Sighişoara – Coşlariu – Phase II" was EUR 3.9 million, with the Cohesion Fund contributing EUR 2.4 million. It is expected that trains running on this renovated section are now able to operate at speeds of 120 to 160 km/h, thus cutting the travel time between the two cities by half. There are plans to rehabilitate train stations located in capital cities as a priority, then those of touristic importance according to the standards set by the EU.

Source: For Warsaw: Luica, P. (2017[58]), "Warsaw makes progress on public transport development", https://www.railwaypro.com/wp/warsaw-makes-progress-public-transport-development/ (accessed on 9 August 2019); For Romania: Thomas, M. (2015[59]), *Romania's General Transport Master Plan and Rail System - In-Depth Analysis*, http://www.europarl.europa.eu/RegData/etudes/IDAN/2015/540376/IPOL_IDA(2015)540376_EN.pdf (accessed on 13 August 2018) and EC (n.d.[60]), "Rail line connects communities in Romania's Centru and Vest regions", http://ec.europa.eu/regional_policy/en/projects/romania/rail-line-connects-communities-in-romanias-centru-and-vest-regions.

Improving and expanding public transport can be challenging due to uncertain long-term financial stability. In order to provide a sustainable and competitive public transport network, constant investments in infrastructure and operation are required and, in most cases, subsidies are necessary to maintain quality and affordability (Aguilar Jaber and Glocker, 2015[61]). In some cities, transport is heavily subsidised under the argument that high subsidies are needed to provide services at affordable prices, as it happens in Mexico City (Table 2.6). In Warsaw, Poland, the public transport system is financed 33% from ticket selling and the rest from the municipal budget (Florczak, 2012[62]). The problem is that subsidies are sometimes established without adequate analysis of costs structures and affordability of tariffs.

Table 2.6. Fares and calculated operating costs of a trip on public transport in Mexico City, 2015

	Price per trip (MXN)	Calculated cost per trip (MXN)
Metro	5.00	11.50
RTP ordinary bus service	2.00	7.50
RTP Ecobus service	5.00	12.00

Source: OECD (2015[26]), *OECD Territorial Reviews: Valle de México, Mexico*, https://dx.doi.org/10.1787/9789264245174-en.

Moreover, in some countries (i.e. Chile, Colombia, Mexico and Poland), the heavy dependence of cities on national fund transfers and the limited tax autonomy of subnational governments limits resources to finance infrastructure. Some cities have developed a greater capacity to generate local funds but have difficulties obtaining the national government's approval to use certain sources of revenue. In Denmark, cities cannot use revenues from congestion charges as they are considered new taxes (Aguilar Jaber and Glocker, 2015[61]). In New South Wales (NSW), Australia, the Independent Pricing and Regulatory Tribunal (IPART) regulates the public transport fares, which limits the amount fares can be increased within a year. The problem for funding is that the government does not always increase the fares to the amount allowed by IPART. According to the NSW government, Sydney public transport fares are relatively low compared to those in London and Munich which are more than double those in Sydney (NSW Government, 2018[12]).

In the Madrid region (CAM), Spain, like in many other regions in the world, the financial sustainability of the transport system seems to be a challenge as over 57% of the income comes from subsidies and only about 43% from user fees (Table 2.7). The regional government is by far the main contributor to the system with 44% of the total spending followed by the city of Madrid and the central state administration. The city councils of the CAM with urban transport services also contribute to the financing but to a much lesser extent.

Table 2.7. Financing of the transport system in the Madrid region

Public subsidies	2016 (EUR millions)	Percentage
Central administration	126.7	5.70
Madrid region (CAM)	980.1	44.11
Madrid City	149.1	6.71
Other cities	14.1	0.63
Total	**1 270.0**	**57.16**
Revenues from fees	952	42.84
Total	**2 222**	**100**

Source: Velasco, A. (2016[4]), *Integration of the Public Transport System in Madrid Region*, Consorcio Regional de Transportes de Madrid, Madrid.

Cities need to ensure co-ordination of investment that comes from different sources (national funds, regional funds, local revenues) and the link between those investment decisions and accessibility strategies. For this purpose, cities need to adopt mechanisms to link national grants to local project implementation according to urban accessibility objectives to avoid a high share of funds being spent on one particular item such as urban roads.

Transport is a priority sector across subnational governments in OECD countries

Transport and economic affairs are the largest sectors of subnational investment in the OECD accounting for almost 40% of the total subnational investment. Under this heading are transport, communications, economic development, energy, construction, etc. Transport systems, facilities and public transport account for around 75% of investment and comprise the construction of roads (highways, local roads, bicycle paths, etc.), railways, water transport, air transport and airports, and even cable cars or funiculars, etc. (OECD, 2018[63]). This level of investment varies across countries from around 50% in Australia, Estonia and Ireland, to less than 20% in Denmark, Latvia, Slovenia and Sweden (Figure 2.9).

At a global level, education, social protection, general public services (mainly administration) and health are the primary areas of subnational government (SNG) spending as a share of GDP and share of SNG expenditure. SNG spending on economic affairs (industry, energy, mining, agriculture and construction) and transportation (roads, public transport, etc.) account for 1.3% of GDP and 13.9% of subnational spending (Table 2.8). Data do not show the difference between the share of economic affairs and transportation but, based on the information from OECD countries, it may be assumed that the largest share is investment in transport. These shares vary between federal (2.8% of GDP and 14.1% of subnational spending) and unitary countries (1.0% of GDP and 13.9% of subnational spending) (OECD/UCLG, 2019[44]).

Table 2.8. Examples of areas of subnational government spending

Areas	Percentage of GDP	Percentage of SNG expenditure
Education	2.6	23.6
Social protection	1.8	12.4
General public services	1.7	18.5
Health	1.5	10.7
Economic affairs and transport	1.3	13.9
Housing and community amenities	0.6	8.0
Recreation, culture and religion	0.5	5.6
Environmental protection	0.3	5.0
Public order and safety and defence	0.3	..

Note: Data are available for 67 countries. .. : no available data.
Source: Elaborated based on OECD/UCLG (2019[44]), "2019 Report World Observatory on Subnational Government Finance and Investment: Key findings", http://www.sng-wofi.org/publications/2019_SNG-WOFI_REPORT_Key_Findings.pdf (accessed on 28 August 2019).

Funding transport investment requires fostering metropolitan co-ordination

One of the first elements to boost cities' investment capacity is to motivate metropolitan co-ordination and co-operation for planning and investment. Co-ordination is particularly relevant in metropolitan areas where there is no metropolitan government but a fragmented administration. Requiring a collaborative long-term planning process for transport project fund eligibility can act as a powerful catalyst for metropolitan-wide concertation (OECD, 2015, p. 35[24]). A lack of co-operation can inhibit investment in fragmented metropolitan areas. For instance, Warsaw's Public Transport Authority (ZTM) provides public transport only within the administrative border of the city but, through bilateral agreements, it is able to extend the service to the metropolitan area despite a lack of metropolitan-wide regulations. Warsaw's strategic documents, such as the transport policy, are not applicable to the 31 communities outside the city area and ZTM cannot invest in those areas due to the lack of metropolitan regulations, despite intermodality and integration requiring investments. Poland's Public Transport Law of 2011 does not recognise the metropolitan area and there are no provisions for financing joint projects nor setting new sources of income. According to the law, only 5 out of 72 municipalities in Warsaw metropolitan area are required to design their own local transport plan. Without co-operation many entities may overlap their jurisdictions (Florczak, 2012[62]).

The US offer an example where metropolitan planning organisations (MPOs) were explicitly created for planning and programming federal transport funds (Box 2.11). The goal was to ensure that existing and future expenditures for transport investment projects were based on a continuing, co-operative and comprehensive planning process. In Île-de-France, local governments and employers, members of *Île-de-France Mobilités*, are responsible for the financing of transport investment through a series of contributions that vary according to the zone in which the municipalities are located. Similarly, financing transport in London requires a combination of different sources of which contributions from the London boroughs and the private sector are necessary. London has the problem of financing transport operating costs in an environment where the population is growing and government grants are falling but still, the city needs to provide an efficient, reliable and affordable service. The delivery of its transport strategy requires the close collaboration of government, national rail, London's boroughs and the private sector.

Figure 2.9. Breakdown of SNG investment by economic function as a share of total SNG investment, 2016

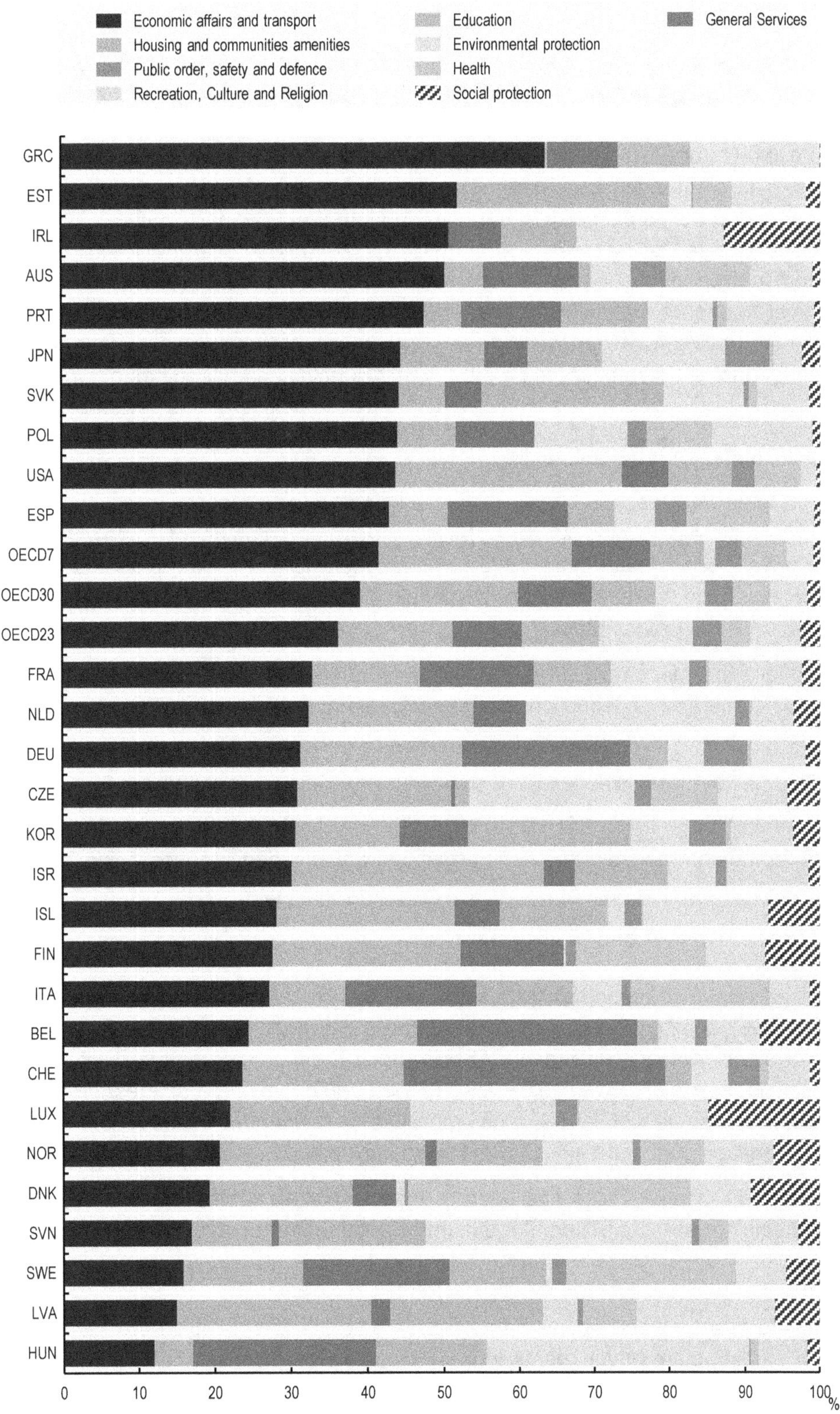

Note: OECD7 refers to federal countries and OECD23 to unitary countries.
Source: OECD (2018[63]), *OECD Regions and Cities at a Glance 2018*, https://dx.doi.org/10.1787/reg_cit_glance-2018-en.

Box 2.11. Supporting metropolitan-wide transport funding

MPOs in the United States

In the US, urban areas of more than 50 000 residents are required to have an MPO to qualify for federal transport funding. In 2013, there were 342 MPOs in the country. The reasons for their creation was to facilitate adaptation to local conditions in order to best allocate federal transport funding. To access federal funding, MPOs need to develop long-range transportation plans with planning horizons of at least 20 years. The plans must be based on demographic, travel and employment trends for their regions and propose a series of transport improvements to meet projected needs. The plans must be elaborated based on a realistic assessment of the available funding over the planning period to avoid transport project to exceed identified revenues. Moreover, every decision must be evaluated against a set of alternatives to ensure that the most cost-effective solutions are chosen. The long-term plans are then translated into rolling five-year transport improvement programmes containing all projects to be funded in the metropolitan area over the next five years, identifying the sources of funding allocated to each.

Funding of public transport in Île-de-France

Public transport in Île-de-France is largely funded by local governments (*communes*) and companies which are members of Île-de-France Mobilités (72%). The transport payment is a tax paid by companies and public or private bodies with more than 11 employees. It is the main resource of Île-de-France Mobilités. This tax is collected by the bodies responsible for collecting social security contributions and then transferred to Île-de-France Mobilités.

Public contributions are mandatory expenses for local authorities that are members of Île-de-France Mobilités. The different rates of deduction for the employers of the communes concerned vary according to the zones:

- 2.95% for zone 1, that includes Paris and Hauts-de-Seine municipalities.
- 2.12% for the municipalities of Seine-Saint-Denis and Val-de-Marne.
- 2.01% for the communes of the Paris urban unit not included in zones 1 and 2.
- 1.6% for Essonne, Seine-et-Marne, Val d'Oise and Yvelines.

Income

Most of the investment income comes from self-financing, proceeds of fines, the loan and balance of the Agency for the Financing of Transport Infrastructures of France grant (*Agence pour le financement des infrastructures de transport de France,* AFITF) under the financing part of the rolling stock in the Paris region. The proceeds of police fines relating to road traffic is an important resource in that it comes directly the investment section of Île-de-France Mobilités. In fact, under Article R. 4414-1 of the general code of local authorities, half of the fines for the region are paid to Île-de-France Mobilités.

Since 2012, Île-de-France Mobilités has been obliged to borrow to finance its investments, its own resources not being sufficient to absorb the dynamics of the different investment projects.

Expenditure

Since 2007, Île-de-France Mobilités has embarked on an ambitious multiyear investment policy which concerns both infrastructure, investments in quality of service (accessibility, passenger information, security, etc.), acquisition and the renovation of rolling stock. Directly or indirectly, Île-de-France Mobilités finances 100% of buses, trains-RER, metros and trams; 66% of direct investment expenditure is allocated to the financing of rolling stock (rail and bus). Infrastructure expansion investments are mainly financed under state-region plan contracts or region-department specific contracts. Intermodality investments are financed by a subsidy from Île-de-France Mobilités and the participation of project owners. Since 2015, the acquisitions of new trains are all entirely subsidised by Île-de-France Mobilités.

Funding public transport in London

Delivering London's transport strategy requires an average capital investment of GBP 3.3 billion a year until 2041. This equates to around 0.9% of London's gross value added (GVA) or 1.2% of GDP per annum. Transport in London is funded through a mix of sources which include:

- Business rate retention (BRR) under mayoral control, which replace existing direct government grants for operations and new capital investment.
- Transport for London (TfL) "prudential borrowing" against future revenue.
- Revenue from fares and other "user pays" sources such as congestion charging.
- Non-fare sources such as advertising and property.
- Contributions from the London boroughs and the private sector, such as developer funding for associated transport investments.
- Other specific grants.

For specific projects, such as the Elizabeth line project, all funds are ring-fenced specifically (i.e. specific levies such as business rate supplements [BRS] and the community infrastructure levy [CIL]). TfL's operating expenditure, including capital renewals, rely mainly on fares and BRR funding sources.

The Transport Strategy foresees that capital grants and prudential borrowing, which funded capital investments in the past, are likely to be scaled down. The strategy considers that additional borrowing will only be an option where the capital spends results in an increase in future revenues that can service the operating and financing costs.

Moreover, future capital spending is expected to be used to deliver the aims of the Healthy Streets Approach highlighted in the Transport Strategy. However, since these types of schemes are generally much cheaper to deliver than large infrastructure schemes, they cannot provide the revenue required to sustain further borrowing. Thus, additional sustainable funding sources and project-specific grants are needed to deliver the Transport Strategy alongside contributions from the boroughs and the private sector.

Source: OECD (2015[24]), *Governing the City*, https://doi.org/10.1787/9789264226500-en (accessed on 9 August 2017).; Île-de-France Mobilités (n.d.[64]), *Le financement des transports publics*, www.iledefrance-mobilites.fr/le-financement-des-transports-publics/ (accessed 17 June 2020); Greater London Authority (2018[13]), *Mayor's Transport Strategy*, http://www.london.gov.uk (accessed on 15 July 2019).

Funding transport requires a focus on spending efficiency

The continuous increase in operational costs and the limited sources of revenue lead cities to adopt a focus on spending efficiency. Costs for maintenance, the expansion of public transport networks and the implementation of safety measures are constantly growing. In New South Wales, Australia, operating costs for public transport grew at 3.4% on average between 2016 and 2018, against an average growth of 1.8% in the period June 2011-June 2016 (NSW Government, 2018[12]). Cities are looking into new technologies to use vehicles that are more environmentally friendly and financially sustainable. This is because fuel is not just a pollutant but also represents a significant percentage of the cost of public transport services.

Construction to improve the public transport network also adds to rising costs. In New South Wales, since 2012, public transport capital investment has grown 13% each year on average. In recent years, a total of

AUD 32 billion[16] has been invested in the network and an additional AUD 50 billion are planned for the next 10 years (NSW Government, 2018[12]).

To recover more of what cities spend in public transport, cities may need to consider introducing commercial approaches to asset ownership including a greater level of scrutiny over funding, performance and efficiency targets and cost constraints. Cities may also need to ensure that all capital investment decisions are based on opportunities to deliver commercial returns on new assets beyond their core transport uses. The inclusion of targets in planning, operation and maintenance contracts will also help to pursue more spending efficiency.

Governmental capacity

To be able to implement their public transport plans and achieve their accessibility objectives, cities should ensure they have the capacity and capability to do so. There are two aspects of governmental capacity in this respect: human capital and data collection for *ex post* assessments.

Cities require highly qualified staff to foster urban accessibility

Attracting and investing in a talented and dedicated workforce in the administration and transport authority is essential to achieve excellence in all aspects of operations. To be effective, cities should ensure that they have the necessary staffing levels and that employees are equipped with the tools and resources necessary to get their jobs done. For this, cities and transport agencies in particular, need to invest in strategic public employment policies that include recruitment, staff development and retention, comprehensive employee training, employee diversity and equal opportunities, work safety and training for managers to manage staff.

The lack of sufficient human capacity and capability at the interior of the local administration may hinder the effectiveness of cities' investment programmes. In many countries, SNGs lack the capacity for managing investment projects. In Romania, for instance, in the municipalities of the central and western regions, the local public workforce does not always have the necessary skills and competencies to conduct strategic planning and manage investment projects. Public employees with skills in strategic planning, project management, the culture of setting partnership, innovation, etc. are needed to increase the know-how of the local administrations. There are capacity-building programmes to support local authorities in public procurement and planning. Lack of data could also be one of the reasons for inefficient planning. For instance, in Sibiu, Romania, concession contracts are granted to private bus operators. The problem is that they do not share data and information on their operations with the municipal government (at least not in a systematic way).

Promoting accessibility requires local cross-disciplinary workforces. Local authorities now recruit fewer staff with specialist technical training for a specific job. People are more trained on the job and move around within the local administration to gain experience in different departments. Research suggests that people with cross-disciplinary experience are often better equipped to deal with the issues of integrating land use, transport and environmental policy as these areas increasingly require an inter-disciplinary perspective (Stead and Geerlings, 2005[30]).

Not all cities include capacity-building measures in their development of transport strategies. This could be a missed opportunity for many cities to clarify and reflect on their staffing needs and plan their workforce strategically. This is particularly important in a moment when city authorities and transport agencies in particular look for ways to increase efficiency in their operations. There is the risk of seeing the workforce as a cost and not as an asset. Without careful planning, cities and transport authorities could be in a situation of dedicating large amounts of time and resources to reskill the workforce, so the actual gains of the efficiency efforts could be minimal.

The New York City (NYC) Department of Transportation (DOT) has a clear strategy for ensuring the capacity for delivering its transport plans. It acknowledges that without staff with the right skills, it may not be able to manage the transport network in an efficient and effective manner. There are three aspects that should be highlighted from this strategy (Box 2.12). First, it considers comprehensive training as a key part of its employees' career development and therefore promotes movements across the different units of the department. Second, it fosters diversity in the workforce by looking to recruit people from different backgrounds and from different parts of the city and, by doing so, the DOT's workforce reflects the society it serves. Finally, it looks into the future by targeting recruitment of future members of staff with the skills and competencies the DOT requires. The experience of the NYC DOT highlights the importance of workforce planning to ensure the capacity and capability of the workforce. Other examples include the transport strategy of the New South Wales (NSW) government which highlights the need to improve the skills and capabilities of the workforce to build collaborative partnerships with customers, community and the private sector (NSW Government, 2018[12]). The experience of the national government of Canada shows that workforce planning has the potential to facilitate the workforce renewal even in times of fiscal restraint through re-purposing/re-deployment of existing staff, and focused recruitment and talent acquisition, even at a reduced level (Huerta Melchor, 2013[65]).

Box 2.12. NYC Department of Transportation – Diversity and rotational programmes

The NYC DOT has nearly 5 000 employees, of which 50% work in the field. As part of its efforts to enhance efficiency and effectiveness in its operations, the DOT has embarked in a programme to prepare the next generation of leaders to ensure that the agency can continue to be effective as veteran DOT staff retire. To replace retiring staff, the agency recruits new members of staff from all parts of the city so that they reflect and understand the diversity of NYC. Currently, the DOT provides training programmes to help employees close gaps in their knowledge which could range from software training to supervisor competencies.

Since 2017, the DOT pilots a rotational programme in which selected DOT employees can do work exchanges with other DOT units and divisions, gaining experience in planning, outreach, design, data analysis and other fields. To ensure diversity in its workforce, the DOT is expanding its outreach efforts to groups underrepresented in the agency. Moreover, the DOT is creating an "ambassador programme" for outreach and recruitment to schools, colleges and universities. For this purpose, the DOT's Recruitment Coordinator works closely with the operating divisions to identify current employees who are recent graduates to expand the pool of individuals who can represent the agency at career fairs and other on-campus recruitment opportunities.

Source: NYC DOT (2016[23]), *New York City Strategic Plan 2016*, https://www.nycdotplan.nyc/PDF/Strategic-plan-2016.pdf (accessed on 6 August 2019).

Developing capacity for data collection and ex post *assessment*

Developing the ability to exploit the power of data is a key factor in improving accessibility and developing long-term transport plans. The provision of accurate, timely and comprehensive data on people's mobility needs can enable city leaders, planners and even citizens and businesses to make decisions that better meet these needs. For instance, the lack of updated data on mobility patterns was one of the key drawbacks of the Transantiago project in Chile, the upgrade of the capital city's public transport system that started in 2007 (see Chapter 1). Centralising information collected by agencies in charge of different modes of transport in each jurisdiction of a metropolitan area is essential for data management. All information can then be used on a metropolitan-wide platform. Data collected by different agencies should be opened up to other agencies, citizens and businesses, and be made easy to aggregate to gain greater insight into city life (BSI, 2015[66]) and in particular transport. The benefits of such an integrated approach are tangible and can be substantial. Data collection should take advantage of future fare integration initiatives to collect information on whole origin-destination travel, rather than trip segments only. Solid models based on long-term population and employment trends could be developed and used to decide on the projects that the transport and accessibility strategies should include. The importance of this data collection and modelling exercise is that it can also guide resource allocation (OECD, 2015[26]).

Box 2.13. Smart traffic management in Stockholm

In Stockholm, Sweden, the KTH Royal Institute of Technology uses streaming analytics technology to gather real-time information from global positioning system (GPS) devices in nearly 1 500 taxi cabs in the city and there are plans to expand it to collect data from delivery trucks, traffic sensors, transit systems, pollution monitors and weather information systems. The data is processed providing real-time information on traffic flow, travel times and the best commuting options.

The city of Stockholm and IBM have been working together to monitor traffic flow during peak hours. The congestion management system has reduced traffic in Stockholm by 20%, average travel times by 50%, emissions by 10% and the proportion of green tax-exempt vehicles has risen to 9%.

Source: BSI (2015[66]), *Smart Cities Overview - Guide*, http://shop.bsigroup.com/upload/Shop/Download/PAS/30313208-PD8100-2015.pdf (accessed on 4 September 2019).

Detailed documentation for conducting *ex post* assessment of projects is needed to build expertise in policy and project implementation. This can help to improve insight into the impact of chosen strategies and indicate any adjustments needed. Cities also develop clear indicators for measuring progress as some transport strategies are evaluated on an annual basis. Annual reports like the ones required by Mexico City's Mobility Law or Malmö's Sustainable Urban Mobility Plan are a useful instrument to follow up the strategies, plans, programmes and actions. Planning, monitoring and *ex post* assessments are tools that should help authorities identify how far transport policies and projects are promoting accessibility and contributing to economic development and well-being. Indicators and assessment methodologies should aim to measure the impact of transport policies on economic development, well-being and accessibility. They should also – ideally – be integrated into a circular fashion where evaluation informs improvements to existing policy and strategy (OECD, 2017[67]). The city of Malmö, for example, has developed a series of indicators as part of its Accessibility Index to support decisions in planning and in weighing different investments and actions (Box 2.14).

Box 2.14. Malmö's Accessibility Index criteria

The Accessibility Index developed by the transport authorities of the city of Malmö, Sweden, constitutes a support for follow up of how accessibility in the transport system develops over time. The criteria included for sustainable accessibility are:

- Travel time by walking to ten destinations.
- Travel time by cycling to ten destinations.
- Travel time ratio bicycle/car to ten destinations.
- Travel time ratio public transport/car to the city centre, nearest commercial area/shopping mall and nearest public transport mode.
- Distance to the nearest bus stop (with good headway).
- Distance to nearest major public transport node.
- Distance to nearest car sharing facility.
- Range of travel opportunities, i.e. access to several sustainable transport modes with good accessibility (freedom of choice).

To follow up on the Sustainable Urban Mobility Plan, Figure 2.10 depicts the documentation and data required for the Accessibility Index:

Figure 2.10. Malmo's documents for a follow-up strategy

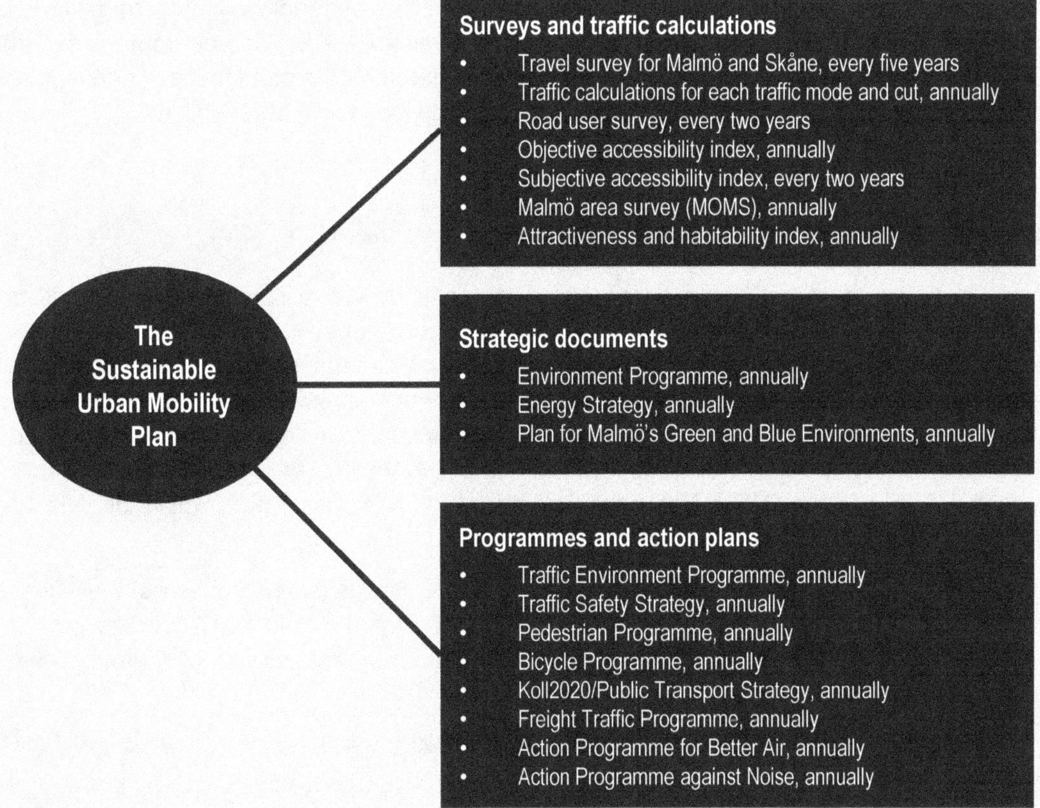

Source: City of Malmö (2016[9]), *Sustainable Urban Mobility Plan: Creating a More Sustainable Malmö*, https://malmo.se/download/18.16ac037b154961d0287384d/1491301288704/Sustainable+urban+mobility+plan%28TROMP%29_ENG.pdf (accessed on 16 July 2019).

Community engagement

Cities and transport authorities view public engagement and customer service as a core component of their transport and accessibility strategies. Major transport projects are increasingly developed in partnership with the local community. Engaging in meaningful dialogue with businesses and inhabitants is one of the elements of the policymaking process and implementation of the transport strategies. According to the OECD Principles on Urban Policy, engaging stakeholders in the design and implementation of urban-related policies, it is essential to involve all segments of society, in particular the most vulnerable residents (i.e. women, the elderly, youth, disabled people and migrants), and to harness innovative mechanisms to engage the private sector (OECD, 2019[15]). Cities need to harness the knowledge of citizens by providing win-win opportunities to gain their active participation in city transformation (BSI, 2015[66]). This can help city leaders to co-ordinate the activities of citizens around common goals. One aspect that government officials need to manage carefully is that of a situation when a transport project generates costs or disruption for the local population. For example, the project proposal for a third runway at London's Heathrow Airport has been long opposed by local residents who already face high levels of noise and pollution and any further expansion will likely exacerbate this.[17] This opposition is despite the economic benefits the capacity expansion of the airport would mean to the national and local economy.

The extent and type of outreach cities and their transport authorities do vary but there is a clear recognition across cities of the importance of community engagement. For example, the NYC DOT organises or participates in hundreds of public meetings a year from workshops to community board presentations. The DOT normally responds to over 30 000 inquiries from elected officials, community boards and the public every year (NYC DOT, 2016[23]). A challenge for political and transport authorities is how to balance or treat the different needs of different social groups when designing transport projects. Citizens have different needs, preferences and opportunities to access various activities depending on several factors such as the stage in life, gender, income and perceptions on what is valuable. A key lesson from the experience of the NYC DOT is that, although community engagement cannot generate consensus, it can help generate more effective projects and programmes that reflect local knowledge and perspectives.

Box 2.15. NYC Department of Transportation – Vision Zero Outreach

Community engagement is included in every aspect or step of the Vision Zero initiative. The Vision Zero Action Plan is the city's foundation for ending traffic deaths and injuries in the streets. In 2014, the DOT partnered with the NY Police Department, Taxi and Limousine Commission (TLC) and elected officials from across the city to hold over 25 Vision Zero town hall meetings and workshops where members of the public were invited to identify safety priorities in their communities. Residents submitted over 10 000 comments on key safety issues through an interactive Vision Zero map on the DOT's website. This feedback informed the DOT's Borough Pedestrian Safety Action Plans, which identifies priority intersections and streets for safety improvements.

Once the DOT developed specific safety actions to address citizens' safety concerns, these plans are in turn shared with local stakeholders, including community boards, civic and advocacy groups, and elected officials. In 2015, the DOT developed 60 Vision Zero projects, all of them developed in partnership with the community.

Source: NYC DOT (2016[23]), *New York City Strategic Plan 2016*, https://www.nycdotplan.nyc/PDF/Strategic-plan-2016.pdf (accessed on 6 August 2019).

Cities are exploring new ways of problem-solving that fit within their vision-led approach to planning. For instance, a key feature in the approach to planning of the government of New South Wales (NSW), Australia, is co-design to foster a high level of collaboration and decision-making. This requires that from the first stages of planning, the NSW government engages all levels of government, customers and industry in discussing critical transport problems and together find innovative solutions (NSW Government, 2018[12]). For that, the Future Transport team visited over 60 regional and metropolitan locations to talk to the community, industry and local councils and directly seek their input. The NSW government and the transport authority led a Future Transport campaign that produced over 10 000 website reactions to the strategy and plans, 2 000 comments and more than 500 submissions. The local government also used social media to engage with young people. This strategy emphasises the importance of involving people in the conversation who use or are affected by the transport network.

There are still local governments that are reluctant to promote community participation in decision-making. Veselý and Vacek (2013[68]) argue, for instance, that most Czech municipalities still distrust participatory processes as they are afraid of civic protests. But it is precisely the lack of participation and information that leads to social dissatisfaction. Unlike other cities in the country, Prague has a strong community engagement tradition for planning. Updating the Strategic Plan for the City of Prague was conducted through a participatory process that included professionals and the public. In-depth interviews, workshops, working groups and consultations were organised to develop a common vision and set the development priorities of the city. Prague's Strategic Plan fosters sustainable urban development through the promotion of creativity, citizens' participation in urban life, enhancing social cohesion and the revitalisation of public spaces. One example is the reconstruction in 2015 of Vinohradská Street where citizens got involved in preparatory works and the improvement of the urban design concept prepared by Prague's Planning Institute (IPR) (OECD, 2018[69]).

In Canada's Metro Vancouver, community engagement is considered a fundamental civic goal to create an engaged city to address issues of common importance, solve shared problems and create positive social change. Community engagement is a way for authorities to obtain people's feedback on refined content and to listen to people's concerns and aspirations on a number of social, economic and urban development related issues. For that purpose, local authorities organise open houses, talk surveys,[18] focus groups, workshops and public hearings. In the City of Vancouver, community engagement processes are defined and communicated from the early stages and the public is welcome to suggest changes to the process in which they are participating. The local authorities ensure that the process has adequate resources (financial and trained staff). Everyone potentially interested in or impacted by an initiative has an opportunity to become involved in the process, although the local government tries to ensure diversity and representation of underrepresented groups. The process has a balance of proactive and reactive techniques to ensure that input is representative and to involve everyone who wants to be. That is why citizens are welcome to address questions to the government directly to planners and submit proposals at their own initiative. The engagement process involves a communication strategy in which media is used regularly to provide general information (which could be available in different languages). The government tries to ensure that the process is as transparent as possible dealing with conflict and imbalances of knowledge in order to maximise participation. There is normally a process of feedback in which local authorities report to participants what they have got from the consultation process and try to reach a decision. This is important because the process addresses both agreements regarding the validity of the facts and understanding of varied opinions and values regarding the outcomes.[19] In the city of Richmond (a municipality within Metro Vancouver), the local government updated its 1999 Official Community Plan in 2009 through extensive participation of residents, business owners, stakeholders (e.g. Richmond School Board, Vancouver International Airport (YVR), Port Metro Vancouver, Metro Vancouver, Urban Development Institute), community groups and the city's advisory committees. The process involved 3 major rounds of community consultation with over 30 public open houses over the 2.5-year period, citywide surveys and online discussion fora. Box 2.16 highlights some of the lessons learnt on community engagement over years of experience that could inform other cities in their consultation processes.

Box 2.16. Lessons learnt on community engagement in Metro Vancouver

To make the most of community engagement in local policymaking, the experience of Metro Vancouver suggests that:

- Authorities should be clear on whether they want to inform or gather input as it is important that citizens are clear from the outset about the objectives of the exercise, as a way to manage expectations.
- Having a good plan determines who can take part and for what reason.
- Once authorities receive feedback from people, when sought after, it is necessary to share it with the community as a whole. Reporting back on what was heard and how it was heard is of the utmost importance to maintain credibility as normally people want to know their feedback was used.
- Government has to take the initiative. To promote citizen participation, local governments need to go to the people, as the latter would never or very seldom approach the government with their ideas or feedback.
- The messages should be simple as people should not feel overwhelmed.
- The use of information and communication technologies (ICTs) is facilitating the interaction between citizens and government, but consultations on line should be quick (2-3 minutes) and short (4 questions maximum).

Source: Interviews with officials in Metro Vancouver.

References

Aguilar Jaber, A. and D. Glocker (2015), "Shifting towards low carbon mobility systems", OECD/ITF, Paris, http://www.internationaltransportforum.org/jtrc/DiscussionPapers/jtrcpapers.html (accessed on 27 August 2019). [61]

Allain-Dupré, D., C. Hulbert and M. Vincent (2017), "Subnational Infrastructure Investment in OECD Countries: Trends and Key Governance Levers", *OECD Regional Development Working Papers*, No. 2017/05, OECD Publishing, Paris, https://dx.doi.org/10.1787/e9077df7-en. [28]

BSI (2015), *Smart Cities Overview - Guide*, BSI, http://shop.bsigroup.com/upload/Shop/Download/PAS/30313208-PD8100-2015.pdf (accessed on 4 September 2019). [66]

City of Gothenburg (2014), *Gothenburg 2035 - Transport Strategy for a Close-Knit City*, Urban Transport Committee, City of Gothenburg, https://goteborg.se/wps/wcm/connect/6c603463-f0b8-4fc9-9cd4-c1e934b41969/Trafikstrategi_eng_140821_web.pdf?MOD=AJPERES (accessed on 16 July 2019). [11]

City of Malmö (2016), *Sustainable Urban Mobility Plan: Creating a More Sustainable Malmö*, City Council of Malmö, https://malmo.se/download/18.16ac037b154961d0287384d/1491301288704/Sustainable+urban+mobility+plan%28TROMP%29_ENG.pdf (accessed on 16 July 2019). [9]

City of Stockholm (n.d.), *Stockholm City Plan*, https://vaxer.stockholm/globalassets/tema/oversiktplan-ny_light/english_stockholm_city_plan.pdf (accessed on 12 July 2019). [19]

CRTM (n.d.), *Conócenos*, https://www.crtm.es/conocenos.aspx. [40]

Duranton, G. and E. Guerra (2016), "Urban accessibility: Balancing land use and transportation", University of Pennsylvania, https://faculty.wharton.upenn.edu/wp-content/uploads/2017/05/Urban-accessibility-Balancing-land-use-and-transportation-Gilles.pdf (accessed on 3 April 2018). [1]

EC (n.d.), "Rail line connects communities in Romania's Centru and Vest regions", European Commission, http://ec.europa.eu/regional_policy/en/projects/romania/rail-line-connects-communities-in-romanias-centru-and-vest-regions. [60]

EC/UN-Habitat (2016), *The State of European Cities 2016 - Cities Leading the Way to a Better Future*, European Commission, http://dx.doi.org/10.2776/770065. [6]

Florczak, M. (2012), "Integration without regulations", https://fsr.eui.eu/wp-content/uploads/121207_Florczak_Maciej.pdf (accessed on 9 August 2019). [62]

Franco, M. (2017), "El Hoy No Circula no es suficiente para combatir la contaminación en Ciudad de México, según un estudio", The New York Times, https://www.nytimes.com/es/2017/02/15/el-hoy-no-circula-no-es-suficiente-para-combatir-la-contaminacion-en-ciudad-de-mexico-segun-un-estudio/ (accessed on 10 September 2019). [25]

García Pastor, A. (2015), "Integration of the public transport system in Madrid region", Consorcio Regional de Transportes de Madrid, Madrid, https://www.slideshare.net/EMBARQNetwork/integration-of-the-public-transport-system-in-madrid-region (accessed on 1 October 2018). [39]

Gil Solá, A., B. Vilhelmson and A. Larsson (2018), "Understanding sustainable accessibility in urban planning: Themes of consensus, themes of tension", *Journal of Transport Geography*, Vol. 70, pp. 1-10, http://dx.doi.org/10.1016/j.jtrangeo.2018.05.010. [10]

Government of British Columbia (1998), *South Coast British Columbia Transportation Authority Act*, http://www.bclaws.ca/civix/document/id/complete/statreg/98030_01#section25 (accessed on 19 March 2020). [56]

Greater London Authority (2018), *Mayor's Transport Strategy*, http://www.london.gov.uk (accessed on 15 July 2019). [13]

Greater Sydney Commission (n.d.), "Sustainability", in *A Metropolis of Three Cities*, https://www.greater.sydney/metropolis-of-three-cities/sustainability (accessed on 3 September 2019). [22]

Harris, J. et al. (2013), "Medium-term budget frameworks in advanced economies: Objectives, design, and performance", in *Public Financial Management and Its Emerging Architecture*, International Monetary Fund, http://dx.doi.org/10.5089/9781475531091.071 (accessed on 4 September 2019). [52]

Huerta Melchor, O. (2013), "The Government Workforce of the Future: Innovation in Strategic Workforce Planning in OECD Countries", *OECD Working Papers on Public Governance*, No. 21, OECD Publishing, Paris, https://dx.doi.org/10.1787/5k487727gwvb-en. [65]

Île-de-France Mobilités (n.d.), *Le financement des transports publics*, http://www.iledefrance-mobilites.fr/le-financement-des-transports-publics/. [64]

Île-de-France Mobilités (n.d.), *Le réseau*, https://www.iledefrance-mobilites.fr/le-reseau/. [32]

IMF (2015), "Romania - Selected issues", No. 15, International Monetary Fund, Washington, DC, http://www.imf.org (accessed on 27 April 2018). [54]

ITF (2018), *How to Make Urban Mobility Clean and Green*, Policy Brief, International Transport Forum, https://www.itf-oecd.org/sites/default/files/docs/cop24-urban-mobility.pdf (accessed on 3 September 2019). [21]

Krakow City (2017), *Krakow Development Strategy - This is Where I Want to Live - Krakow 2030*, http://file:///C:/Users/emore/AppData/Local/Temp/212318_0.pdf. [17]

Kumar, A. and O. Agarwal (2013), *Institutional Labyrinth - Designing a Way Out for Improving Urban Transport Services: Lessons from Current Practice*, World Bank Group, Washington, DC, http://documents.worldbank.org/curated/en/903181468346145008/pdf/840660WP0Insti00Box382110B00PUBLIC0.pdf (accessed on 28 August 2019). [31]

Luica, P. (2017), "Warsaw makes progress on public transport development", Railway PRO, https://www.railwaypro.com/wp/warsaw-makes-progress-public-transport-development/ (accessed on 9 August 2019). [58]

Lukeš, M., M. Kotek and M. Růžička (2014), "Transport demands in suburbanized locations", *Agronomy Research*, Vol. 12/2, pp. 351-358, http://agronomy.emu.ee/vol122/2014_2_6_b5.pdf (accessed on 28 November 2018). [3]

Makovšek, D. (2019), "The role of private investment in transport infrastructure", *ITF Working Group Papers*, International Transport Forum, Paris, http://www.itf-oecd.org (accessed on 23 July 2020). [53]

Mayors' Council on Regional Transportation (2017), *Regional Transportation Investments - A Vision for Metro Vancouver*, https://tenyearvision.translink.ca/downloads/10%20Year%20Vision%20for%20Metro%20Vancouver%20Transit%20and%20Transportation.pdf (accessed on 29 March 2018). [18]

Medda, F. (2012), "Land value capture finance for transport accessibility: A review", *Journal of Transport Geography*, Vol. 25, pp. 154-161, http://dx.doi.org/10.1016/j.jtrangeo.2012.07.013. [47]

Metro Vancouver Regional District (2011), *Regional Growth Strategy - Metro Vancouver 2040: Shaping Our Future*, http://www.metrovancouver.org/services/regional-planning/PlanningPublications/RGSAdoptedbyGVRDBoard.pdf (accessed on 5 April 2018). [34]

Municipality of Madrid (2014), *Plan de movilidad Urbana Sostenible de la ciudad de Madrid*, Ayuntamiento de Madrid, Madrid, https://www.madrid.es/UnidadesDescentralizadas/UDCMovilidadTransportes/MOVILIDAD/PMUS_Madrid_2/PMUS%20Madrid/Plan%20de%20Movilidad%20de%20Madrid%20aprobacion%20final.pdf (accessed on 17 October 2018). [20]

Ngo, V. (2012), "Identifying areas for transit-oriented development in Vancouver using GIS", *Trail Six: An Undergraduate Journal of Geography*, pp. 91-102. [16]

NSW Government (2018), *Future Transport Strategy 2056*, Transport for NSW, Sydney, https://future.transport.nsw.gov.au/sites/default/files/media/documents/2018/Future_Transport_2056_Strategy.pdf. [12]

NYC DOT (2016), *New York City Strategic Plan 2016*, Department of Transportation, New York, https://www.nycdotplan.nyc/PDF/Strategic-plan-2016.pdf (accessed on 6 August 2019). [23]

NYC DOT (n.d.), *About*, https://www1.nyc.gov/html/dot/html/about/about.shtml. [41]

OECD (2019), *Making Decentralisation Work: A Handbook for Policy-Makers*, OECD Multi-level Governance Studies, OECD Publishing, Paris, https://dx.doi.org/10.1787/g2g9faa7-en. [46]

OECD (2019), *OECD Principles on Urban Policy*, OECD, Paris, http://www.oecd.org/cfe/ (accessed on 16 March 2020). [15]

OECD (2018), *Maintaining the Momentum of Decentralisation in Ukraine*, OECD Multi-level Governance Studies, OECD Publishing, Paris, https://dx.doi.org/10.1787/9789264301436-en. [57]

OECD (2018), *OECD Environmental Performance Reviews: Czech Republic 2018*, OECD Environmental Performance Reviews, OECD Publishing, Paris, https://dx.doi.org/10.1787/9789264300958-en. [69]

OECD (2018), *OECD Regions and Cities at a Glance 2018*, OECD Publishing, Paris, https://dx.doi.org/10.1787/reg_cit_glance-2018-en. [63]

OECD (2017), *Gaps and Governance Standards of Public Infrastructure in Chile: Infrastructure Governance Review*, OECD Publishing, Paris, https://doi.org/10.1787/9789264278875-en. [50]

OECD (2017), "Making policy evaluation work: The case of regional development policy", *OECD Science, Technology and Industry Policy Papers*, No. 38, OECD Publishing, Paris, https://dx.doi.org/10.1787/c9bb055f-en. [67]

OECD (2017), *OECD Urban Policy Reviews: Kazakhstan*, OECD Urban Policy Reviews, OECD Publishing, Paris, https://dx.doi.org/10.1787/9789264268852-en. [5]

OECD (2017), *Urban Transport Governance and Inclusive Development in Korea*, OECD Publishing, Paris, https://dx.doi.org/10.1787/9789264272637-en. [42]

OECD (2016), *OECD Territorial Reviews: The Metropolitan Region of Rotterdam-The Hague, Netherlands*, OECD Territorial Reviews, OECD Publishing, Paris, https://dx.doi.org/10.1787/9789264249387-en. [29]

OECD (2016), *Road Infrastructure, Inclusive Development and Traffic Safety in Korea*, OECD Publishing, Paris, https://dx.doi.org/10.1787/9789264255517-en. [43]

OECD (2015), *Governing the City*, OECD Publishing, Paris, https://doi.org/10.1787/9789264226500-en (accessed on 9 August 2017). [24]

OECD (2015), *OECD Territorial Reviews: Valle de México, Mexico*, OECD Territorial Reviews, OECD Publishing, Paris, https://dx.doi.org/10.1787/9789264245174-en. [26]

OECD (2012), *OECD Territorial Reviews: The Chicago Tri-State Metropolitan Area, United States 2012*, OECD Territorial Reviews, OECD Publishing, Paris, https://dx.doi.org/10.1787/9789264170315-en. [55]

OECD (n.d.), *Mobilising Private Investment in Sustainable Transport Infrastructure*, OECD, Paris, https://www.oecd.org/env/cc/financing-transport-brochure.pdf (accessed on 27 August 2019). [51]

OECD/UCLG (2019), "2019 Report World Observatory on Subnational Government Finance and Investment: Key findings", http://www.sng-wofi.org/publications/2019_SNG-WOFI_REPORT_Key_Findings.pdf (accessed on 28 August 2019). [44]

Olajide, O. and M. Arcé (2017), "Funding wisely: Unlocking urban transit with Land Value Capture", KPMG Global, https://home.kpmg/xx/en/home/insights/2017/05/funding-wisely-unlocking-urban-transit-with-land-value-capture.html (accessed on 29 August 2019). [48]

ORR (n.d.), *Who We Work With – Governments*, Office of Road and Rail, https://orr.gov.uk/about-orr/who-we-work-with/government/transport-for-london. [33]

Reschovsky, A. (2019), "The tax autonomy of local governments in the United States", Working Paper WP19AR1, Lincoln Institute of Land Policy, https://www.lincolninst.edu/sites/default/files/pubfiles/reschovsky_wp19ar1.pdf (accessed on 29 August 2019). [45]

Rode, P. et al. (2014), "Accessibility in cities: Transport and urban form", *NCE Cities Paper*, No. 3, LSE Cities, London School of Economics and Political Science, http://www.lsecities.net (accessed on 9 July 2019). [2]

Rodrigue, J. (2020), "The financing of transport infrastructure", in *The Geography of Transport Systems*, Routledge, New York, https://transportgeography.org/?page_id=8689 (accessed on 27 August 2019). [49]

ROPID (2018), *Prague Integrated Transport and ROPID*, ROPID, Prague. [37]

ROPID (n.d.), *We Introduce ROPID*, http://stary.ropid.cz/info/we-introduce-ropid__s219x902.html. [38]

Salat, S. and G. Ollivier (2017), *Transforming the Urban Space through Transit-Oriented Development: The 3V Approach*, World Bank, Washington, DC, https://openknowledge.worldbank.org/handle/10986/26405 (accessed on 10 September 2019). [14]

SEMOVI (2019), *Plan estratégico de movilidad de la Ciudad de México 2019 : una ciudad, un sistema*, Secretaría de Movilidad, Mexico City, https://semovi.cdmx.gob.mx/storage/app/media/uploaded-files/plan-estrategico-de-movilidad-2019.pdf (accessed on 22 July 2020). [7]

Stead, D. and H. Geerlings (2005), "Integrating transport, land use planning and environment policy", *Innovation: The European Journal of Social Science Research*, Vol. 18/4, pp. 443-453, http://dx.doi.org/10.1080/13511610500384194. [30]

Thomas, M. (2015), *Romania's General Transport Master Plan and Rail System - In-Depth Analysis*, European Parliament, http://www.europarl.europa.eu/RegData/etudes/IDAN/2015/540376/IPOL_IDA(2015)540376_EN.pdf (accessed on 13 August 2018). [59]

TransLink (2013), *Regional Transportation Strategy: Strategic Framework*, TransLink, Vancouver, https://www.translink.ca/-/media/Documents/plans_and_projects/regional_transportation_strategy/rts_strategic_framework_07_31_2013.pdf?la=en&hash=0A459174FB44A8870D00EFCE54124A01078D0698 (accessed on 29 March 2018). [35]

TransLink (n.d.), *Learn More About Us*, https://www.translink.ca/About-Us.aspx. [36]

Transport for London (2018), *Cycling Action Plan*, Transport for London, London, http://content.tfl.gov.uk/cycling-action-plan.pdf (accessed on 3 September 2019). [27]

Trejo Nieto, A., J. Niño Amezquita and M. Vasquez (2018), "Governance of metropolitan areas for delivery of public services in Latin America: The cases of Bogota, Lima and Mexico City", *Region*, Vol. 5/3, pp. 49-73, http://dx.doi.org/10.18335/region.v5i3.224. [8]

Velasco, A. (2016), *Integration of the Public Transport System in Madrid Region*, Consorcio Regional de Transportes de Madrid, Madrid. [4]

Veselý, M. and L. Vacek (2013), "To the problems of revitalization of public spaces in Eastern Bloc housing estates", *Journal of Architecture and Urbanism*, Vol. 37/3, pp. 165-172, http://dx.doi.org/10.3846/20297955.2013.841332. [68]

Notes

[1] For further information, see Nikkei Asia, https://asia.nikkei.com/Economy/China-leans-on-auto-subsidies-to-jump-start-post-virus-economy.

[2] Idem.

[3] For further information, see *Lineamientos para la Operación del Fondo Metropolitano para el ejercicio fiscal 2019*, https://dof.gob.mx/nota_detalle.php?codigo=5551141&fecha=26/02/2019.

[4] Opportunity Area Planning Framework (OAPF) refers to the strategic spatial plans for opportunity areas identified as those that can accommodate large-scale development to provide substantial number of new

jobs and houses with a mixed and intense use of land, assisted by good public transport accessibility (Greater London Authority, 2018[13]).

[5] For further information, see https://www.worldbank.org/en/topic/transport/publication/transforming-the-urban-space-through-transit-oriented-development-the-3v-approach.

[6] For further information, see Presidencia de la República de Colombia, https://id.presidencia.gov.co/Paginas/prensa/2019/Presidente-Duque-lanza-Estrategia-Nacional-Movilidad-Electrica-Sostenible-calidad-aire-transporte-eficiente-190828.aspx.

[7] For further information see: OECD (2020), *Metropolitan Areas [database]*, https://doi.org/10.1787/data-00531-en (accessed 15 June 2020).

[8] Metro Vancouver is a partnership of 21 municipalities, 1 electoral area and 1 Treaty First Nation that collaboratively plans for and delivers regional-scale services, http://www.metrovancouver.org/.

[9] For further information, see www.oecd.org/regional/regional-policy/profile-Romania.pdf.

[10] In Vancouver metropolitan area, the Mayors' Council is composed of representatives from each of the 21 municipalities within the transportation service region, as well as electoral area "A" and the Tsawwassen First Nation, and collectively represent the viewpoints and interests of the citizens of the region. For further information, see https://www.translink.ca/About-Us/Governance-and-Board/Mayors-Council.aspx.

[11] A medium-term budget framework (MTBF) refers to the "institutional arrangements in the budget process governing the requirement to present certain medium-term financial information at specific times, procedures for making multiyear forecasts and plans for revenue and expenditure, and obligations to set numerical expenditure limits beyond the annual budget horizon", www.elibrary.imf.org/view/IMF071/20033-9781475531091/20033-9781475531091/ch04.xml?lang=en&redirect=true.

[12] AUD 2 billion equals approximately USD 1.4 billion.

[13] CAD 7 billion equals approximately USD 5.2 billion.

[14] For further information, see Île-de-France Mobilités, www.iledefrance-mobilites.fr/le-financement-des-transports-publics/.

[15] Presentation given by Chile's Ambassador, Felipe Morandé, to the International Transport Forum on 5 September 2019.

[16] AUD 32 billion equals approximately USD 22.7 billion.

[17] For further information, see London Assembly, https://www.london.gov.uk/press-releases/assembly/no-third-runway-at-heathrow.

[18] A survey conducted using digital technologies in which the participant listens to the questions and uses a tablet to answer them.

[19] For further information, see City of Vancouver, https://vancouver.ca/your-government/how-we-do-community-engagement.aspx#spectrum.

www.ingramcontent.com/pod-product-compliance
Lightning Source LLC
LaVergne TN
LVHW080020110826
845148LV00019B/1083
* 9 7 8 9 2 6 4 9 3 9 5 9 2 *